Chasing the Dragons

CHASING THE DRAGONS

Mike Mulloy

Chasing the Dragons
ISBN 1 901442 02 0

First published in 1997 by Pharaoh Press
01344 884436
This edition published in 1998

Typeset in Sabon by Kestrel Data, Exeter, Devon.

Printed in Great Britain by Short Run Press Ltd, Exeter, Devon.

Dedication

To Carol for the sacrifices she was prepared to make over many years to be a policeman's wife and for the courage and support she gave me when adversity came. This is, in so many ways, her story also.

Acknowledgements

The enthusiasm and dedication to duty of every officer of the squad was an outstanding achievement which brought down so many of those who sought to bring misery to the streets with the dealing of hard drugs, the peddlars of death. All of those young lads and girls who served with the squad can be proud of what they did. The forward thinking of Richard Adams took policing into a new aspect.

In this book all the incidents and events occurred as described but the names of those arrested have been changed and bear no resemblance to any party.

I would like to acknowledge my sister Imelda, and my long time partners Tom Hall and Mike Johnson for their encouragement with this book in the early stages, and all of our friends who helped Carol and I throughout the Squad days. The pressure was on both of us and they understood.

Lastly, John O'Toole, of my publishers, whose interest, belief and eventual cajoling brought this book to completion.

FOREWORD

The formation of the Wirral Crime Squad in the summer of 1984 was a direct result of public disquiet. The relatively new (then) phenomena of open and blatant drug dealing from houses and flats in residential areas caused widespread outrage. Not only local people, but their elected councillors, public officials, local newspapers and radio and TV programmes increasingly described the problem and the apparent inability and sometimes unwillingness of the police to 'do something' about it. It was almost impossible as a senior police officer to go to any public meeting without the question of drug dealing being raised, with the inevitable follow up comments on a seeming lack of police response.

This disquiet found fertile ground within the police force, too, particularly among operational officers at street level who could see the problem in their everyday duties. Unfortunately, the structure of most police forces makes it very difficult to react quickly to major social change. There are so many problems, spread over so many areas twenty-four hours a day, seven days a week. The Wirral Division of the Merseyside Police was no exception. There were about 600 police men and women with more than 100 civilian support staff to police more than 330,000 people. This may seem more than sufficient, but Merseyside was an area of higher than average crime and violence rates. The demands of twenty-four hour patrol and response policing left little margin for experiments.

My decision to commit more than thirty officers in one division to deal full-time with drug dealing and the inevitable criminal offshoots of burglary and violence was not universally popular with all my colleagues. However, the results described in this book by Mike Mulloy speak for themselves. As a direct result of their activities, drug dealing and crime on the Wirral was greatly reduced. The relationship between the public and the police was transformed within a matter of months. I have not known anywhere, before or since, such widespread and active public support for local police actions.

However, the problem of illegal drug use and dealing is still with us and not only on the Wirral, but in every advanced western nation. There is no easy answer, but firm and responsible policing is part of the solution. This book describes that most vividly. It is a chronicle of great courage and determination, of dynamic leadership, of common sense and humour. I hope those reading it gain much enjoyment and insight.

Richard Adams QPM MA(Oxon)
Retired Deputy Chief Constable, West Midlands Police
Former Assistant Chief Constable, Merseyside Police

1

Tuesday
31 July 1984

I sat at my desk and read again the memo left for my attention. The divisional chief superintendent, Richard Adams, had ordered me to report to his office at 2pm the following afternoon. Pondering for a moment on the nature of the order, I conceded that speculation was pointless and put the note to one side.

As a uniformed Inspector, I was responsible for a section of officers in Birkenhead. Although somewhat dominated by the sprawling mass of Liverpool on the opposite bank of the River Mersey, the town still flourished with busy shopping centres and a volatile night-life.

Having already taken the night parade with my sergeants, I spent an hour on the reams of paperwork that filtered through my office and then decided to take a mobile tour of the area. In the company of Sgt Stan Preston, a hard-working Geordie, we were having a quiet night until news of an attempted burglary came over the radio. Two men had been disturbed trying to force the patio doors of a property off Bidston Road in Oxton.

Within minutes we arrived at the address and found the occupants badly shaken. As an elderly couple, they were fortunate to have discovered the intruders when they did. Burglaries are not usually discovered until the morning and we had attended several houses in the preceding weeks where a kitchen pan had been left to burn dry on the cooker.

This mystery wasn't resolved until one culprit was arrested and revealed that after gaining access the housebreaker would boil a pan of water and have at his disposal a dreadful weapon should he be disturbed.

The couple were able to give good descriptions and it came as no surprise when I heard of another similar incident nearby. This had been a developing trend. Previously, when a crime had been interrupted, the perpetrator would quickly distance himself from the scene. Now, an increasing number of thieves were drug addicts and so badly in need of cash that when thwarted at one address they would immediately look for another.

I called additional officers into the area by radio as more reports were received. We were dealing with two desperate young addicts, but the next few hours proved to be frustrating. Although never more than a few minutes from each call, the pair continued to evade us. As dawn broke, there had been no recent sightings and no calls from members of the public for more than an hour. Reluctantly, I returned the officers to their regular patrols.

Stan suggested it might be an idea to cruise the area and I agreed. We drove around for an hour and were giving thought to early breakfast, when all such thoughts were banished from our minds. Turning from Upton Road into Park Road West, I glanced to my left. There they were. Two men precisely fitting the given descriptions were leaving the driveway of a semi-detached property and exchanging furtive glances. On seeing the car, they immediately turned and ran back towards the house.

After alerting the Control Room, we abandoned the car and set off after them. Crashing through shrubbery, they scaled a garden wall and disappeared into the property next door. We chased as best we could but, slowed by cumbersome uniforms, struggled to keep up. I've never doubted that a villain being pursued by police officers could set Olympic-qualifying times over short distances. Their luck, however, did not hold out.

A couple of police cars were speeding through Birkenhead Park to our assistance and as the two men cleared another wall, they dropped into the park and into the path of one of the vehicles. One was arrested straight away and the other, unable to outrun a Ford Escort over open ground, was caught a few minutes later. Both were taken to Birkenhead Police Station and lodged in the cells.

Back in the canteen, I took a quick sandwich with Stan as the night was far from over. The arrested men had to be interviewed and the stolen goods found in their possession itemised and logged. The men were brothers from the north end of the town and both had a string of previous convictions. Their story was a familiar one. The eldest admitted to breaking into dozens of homes over the previous three months in order to support a heroin habit costing in excess of £100 a day.

For a few years I had witnessed a growth in drug-related crime. The large council estates contained many high-rise blocks and some were so unpopular that a rapid turnover in tenants was inevitable. The housing policy at the time was to offer the vacant flats to young people, effectively increasing the presence of drug abuse. Decent families moved out and slowly the blocks became drug-infested nests of lawlessness. Part of the task of reclaiming such areas fell to the police but the problem was widespread and it was soon apparent that no geographical boundaries could define areas of abuse; addicts came from a range of social backgrounds.

Crimes of theft had been steadily on the increase. 1981 saw a rise of some 25%, in 1982 they rose by 15% and by a further 12% the following year. As more people were being arrested, a significant number were claiming heroin addiction as their motive for crime. Clearly, we were facing an unprecedented problem in community policing.

The most popular method for taking the drug was known as 'chasing the dragon'. The powdered substance was placed in silver foil and heated. The diamorphine in the fumes was then inhaled through a 'snorting' tube. A gramme of well-diluted heroin would provide the addict with about a dozen 'snorts' and cost, in 1984, about £70. Thus, it didn't take long to develop a habit only sustained criminal activity could support.

At this time, the Merseyside Police Drug Squad consisted of just eleven officers, itself an indication of how the cancer of drug abuse had spread beyond the remedial measures of operational planning. Occasional bursts of police activity were short-lived and largely ineffective, but the Squad's senior officers were still reluctant to acknowledge the link between rising crime rates and drug abuse. When confronted with the collated testimonies of nearly a hundred arrested addicts, it was suggested the figures were inflated by non-abusers seeking to obtain leniency from the courts. If this was true, then the Wirral was blessed with an abundance of talented young thespians; their profuse sweating, intense shaking and repeated vomiting certainly fooled me.

Officially, there were 497 registered drug addicts on Merseyside at the end of 1983. I knew of more 'junkies' in Birkenhead alone. Further evidence of scale was provided by the medical profession. GPs and hospital staff had been inundated with requests for help from the parents of addicted teenage children. Young women were giving birth to heroin-addicted babies. It is nearly ten years since I heard them, but their tormented screams are with me still.

The two Oxton housebreakers were charged to appear before the courts the following morning. I finally left the station with Stan at midday, several hours after our tour was due to finish.

It was only as I crossed the car park I remembered I was due to see the Divisional Chief superintendent in less than two hours' time.

2

Sitting in Molly Hooper's office, I stifled a yawn as I waited to see Richard Adams. I'd been awake for nearly twenty-four hours and Molly Hooper, his secretary, handed me another cup of coffee in sympathy. As was the normal practice, I probed her for clues as to why I had been summoned, but Richard's secretary parried me with her usual aplomb.

Having been at Birkenhead for six years, I idly wondered if I was to be posted. I was happy where I was, but knew from my time in the force to take nothing for granted. I joined the Liverpool City Police in 1960 and became a detective constable with the CID five years later. In my time, I'd served with the Regional Crime Squad, Serious Crime Squad and on countless murder and robbery enquiries, rising to the rank of detective inspector by 1974. In the same year, Liverpool was amalgamated with other local forces to become the Merseyside Police. In 1978, I returned to uniform and was posted to Birkenhead.

Richard didn't keep me waiting long and on entering his office I was also greeted by his deputy, Jim Heaney. After exchanging the usual pleasantries, we spent a few minutes discussing the earlier arrests, a conversation which brought Richard neatly to the reason I'd been called in.

"I'll come straight to the point, Mike," he said, looking at me quite intensely, "I'm concerned about the level of drugs in circulation in this division."

"So am I, Sir," I replied.

"You know it's getting worse. Even national television refers to Birkenhead as 'Smack City'!" He was right. This crude but descriptive term had been in tabloid circulation for a few months. "Obviously, drugs are an issue all over the country, but my concerns and responsibilities are here. Mike, I want something done about it." He stood up and walked over to the window, looking down on the street. "The day before yesterday, I called a special conference of senior officers and outlined the way I intend to deal with the problem. The Central Drug Squad just don't have the resources to tackle drug abuse all over Merseyside and, in any case, crimes involving drugs are inextricably linked with those of robbery and violence. I want the problem tackled on our own doorstep . . . independently."

Not for the first time, I felt Richard had his finger on the pulse. In assessing the situation, his perspective was three-dimensional; the abuse of illegal drugs was socially deep-rooted, demographically widespread and rapidly escalating. I had long ago recognised that drugs should no longer be dealt with in isolation and I was encouraged to hear Richard moving in this direction.

"At the conference, I declared my intention to form a new squad. From next week, the Burglary Squad and the Plain Clothes Department will merge and become the Wirral Crime Squad. There will be additional postings from the CID. The Division's resources are, as you know, limited and I believe this is the most effective way to utilise them." I was impressed. This was innovative and pragmatic policing at its best. I was also more than mildly curious as to what part I was to play in Richard's plans. He continued.

"My expectations of this new squad will be high and, in the final analysis, success will be measured in the number of convictions. To enter into this anything but whole-hearted would be to doom the project to failure from the start. Therefore, I am prepared to commit to it the manpower I think it merits and to do so immediately. The squad will consist of twenty-eight officers, four sergeants and will be led by an inspector." Richard looked at me. "I would like that inspector to be you, Mike."

Earlier in the year, I had been overlooked for the position of commanding the Burglary Squad, so I was flattered to be offered a posting with more responsibility. This divisional squad would be nearly three times the size of the Central Drug Squad. Richard went on to explain that each officer would serve with the squad for six months, after which time they would return to their own sections and pass on the benefit of their experience.

I thought the whole project had been well thought out and said so. I did, however, have one reservation. In order to operate effectively, the squad would need a free-hand when chasing over the four sub-divisions under Richard's command. I envisaged being caught up in endless telephone requests for clearance when moving from one area to another. I asked if that had been considered.

"It has, Mike. Within the division, you will have complete autonomy, reporting only to myself and Mr Heaney here." I was promised the same conditions as other officers, so in six months would be free to return to my own section in Birkenhead. I was excited by this opportunity as nothing on such a scale had been attempted before by the officers of one division. It was, however, a huge undertaking and not for the faint-hearted. I would have to handle each situation as I saw it and stand or fall on my own judgement; there was nobody upon whose experience I could draw. I asked Richard if I could have twenty-four hours to discuss his offer with my wife, Carol.

"Of course, Mike," he said, standing up and giving me his hand, "call me tomorrow."

I've known Carol since we were teenagers and I joined the police force while we were still courting. She was well aware this command would mean long hours, an unpredictable social life and a husband totally commited to the job in hand. For the past six years we had enjoyed as stable a married life as any police officer and his wife could expect and now I was asking her to once again endure the socially disruptive influence of squad work. She recognised, though, how keen I was to take it and it was, after all, only for six months.

She gave me her full support and the following morning I telephoned Richard to give him my decision.

"I expected nothing else, Mike," he said, "but I'm very pleased." We discussed the matter further and went over the arrangements we would have to make for the next few days. "One more thing," Richard added as I was about to hang up, "do you know Miller from the north end?"

3

The squad was based at the divisional head-
quarters in Manor Road, Wallasey, a modern
station with good facilities. It was also well
situated, being close to both the Criminal
Collators' Office and the division's radio control
room. The conference room was given over to the
squad's constables and I based myself along with
my four sergeants in the old offices of the Plain
Clothes Department. It was a little claustrophobic,
but I was satisfied it was good enough for our
purposes. It was, in any case, my intention to have
the squad spend as much time as possible in the
field.

The allocated space was adequate, but we
were sadly lacking in basic office furniture and
equipment and resolving this became our first
operation. Ably led by DC Arthur Cowley,
the squad members swarmed over the station

in search of our requirements.

Before long, we were adequately furnished and before very much longer the complaints started. The first came from the custody sergeant.

"Any of your lads been near the interview room, Sir?" he asked.

"Bloody hell, George! We've only been here five minutes, we haven't pulled anybody yet!"

"Yes, very good, Sir," he acknowledged without a hint of humour. "It's just that two of my lads have been up there with a prisoner and found a tape recorder and a telephone."

"So what?"

"Well, that's all they found, Sir. The table and chairs have gone."

"I'll look into it, George."

"If you would, Sir."

A short while later, Arthur was caught red-handed removing chairs from, of all places, the office of the Force Discipline and Complaints Against Police Section at an adjacent station.

He had to put them back, but beat a hasty retreat before they missed the typewriter. I reeled him in when I received a call from Richard asking me to explain why Arthur was in his office with a tape measure. In this way we managed to equip ourselves and if we ruffled a few feathers, I felt our needs were greatest.

The other major problem of logistics was transport. We were issued with just two vehicles, both practically useless for our purposes. One was a bright green Vauxhall with the number plate 'HAT 123Y' and already fondly referred to by the area's criminal fraternity as Hatty. The other was a Mini Metro with its radio mounted proudly on top of the dashboard. I sent the Metro back to Workshops to have the radio resited, but we kept the Vauxhall.

"We can use it for goin' to the chippy," Arthur dryly suggested.

When the Metro came back a few days later, my request to conceal the radio had been taken literally. It was now fixed under the passenger seat and could only be used if the car was stopped and the seat raised. Our problem was finally resolved by DC Frank Anderson and a few other lads who acquired the necessary vehicles from a variety of imaginative sources. I watched in bemused admiration as hire cars, council vehicles and Manweb vans rolled into the station, all borrowed on the strength of a phone call or two. Those senior officers who raised an eyebrow assumed somebody somewhere had authorised it. As Richard had promised, we were left very much to our own devices.

Towards the end of the first morning, I called the squad together to discuss our *modus operandi*. We were in receipt of a considerable amount of disjointed information, gleaned from both the public and interviewed suspects. Before our arrival, there had been insufficient manpower and resources to co-ordinate an effective response. We were there to provide one. I wanted to pursue a policy of 'in your face' policing.

It was immediately clear that the supply and distribution of class-A drugs, such as heroin, cocaine, LSD and some amphetamines, was organised, but it wasn't yet possible to identify a coherent structured network. There had been a general belief among senior CID officers that the Wirral, unlike many parts of Liverpool, had not been syndicated by local gangs. My first impression was that it probably had. I recognised names from the armed gangs of the seventies whose very existence was protected by long-standing structured organisations. I also thought it significant that despite the enormous financial rewards of drug-dealing, there was a conspicuous absence of territorial conflict. I felt that only a mafia-style network could control such inter-gang activities without warfare.

The squad was set to further assimilate the information we held and I retired to my office where I was joined by my sergeants: Bob Hughes, 'Elly' Davies, Dave Ackerley and Mike Carr. Our first task was to organise the squad into four teams and each of them made requests to have specific officers in their own team. I stressed upon them the need to apply sustained and intensive pressure on our targets and I was determined that from 'Day One' our methods should be carefully co-ordinated and acceptable to all staff members. Those who were not totally committed to the task and the methods we would employ would be returned to their sections. If we were to make an impression we would need to be unorthodox, determined and undivided.

Mike Carr was one of the few officers I had with any practical experience in pursuing drug dealers and voiced his concern over what co-operation we could expect from within the force. I reminded him that we had the run of the division and that I didn't anticipate any obstructions.

"There'll be some," he insisted, "when we apply for search warrants."

"Why?"

"If we want a warrant for a suspected dealer, we have to go through the Central Drug Squad in Liverpool."

"Yeah, well, we can't be doing that every five minutes. In future, if the raid is on the Wirral, we'll just go ahead and do it. If we have to go over to Liverpool, we'll let them know. If any flak comes back, refer them to me." This met with general approval and Mike smiled broadly.

"Nice one, Boss."

As it turned out, we did hear a few noises from Liverpool, but not for long. I saw Richard daily and was well aware of his influence behind the scenes. To be fair, the Drug Squad were ridiculously undermanned for the task it was set. Their officers had developed methods based on the limited resources at their disposal. I could sympathise, but I couldn't be deflected.

There were essentially three points I considered vital in exploiting the maximum initial impact: objecting to bail on all charges of supply; the meticulous taping of all interviews with suspects; and the use of forced entry on the majority of drug raids.

In the past, once recovered drugs were submitted to forensics for analysis, the arrested man was released on bail and within a short time would be back on the street dealing. Richard and I wanted this stopped and intended using the influence of my rank to object to bail at court hearings. It was important that dealers recognised arrest as more than a minor inconvenience.

The formal taping of all interviews was not at this time standard practice. Fortunately, stations on the Wirral had been part of Home Office trials, so all the necessary equipment was in place. This was a valuable tool in securing convictions, especially if a written confession was later withdrawn.

My insistence on forced entry was based on both the desire to surprise the targets, so denying them the opportunity to flush the drugs away before we gained access, and to send out a clear message to dealers throughout the division that we meant business. I wanted dealers to live in a constant state of fear and apprehension.

I held a final conference with the staff before I let them loose on an unsuspecting public. Few of them were known to me personally, but they were keen and each and every one of them had volunteered for this assignment. The joke circulating on the day was that they been threatened with the option of dismissal and a few had chosen to pick up their P45s. I was Lee Marvin and the squad were the Dirty Dozen!

It was important to me that they wanted to be there. Within a few weeks they would be long-haired, unshaven and dressed in old jeans and sweatshirts to blend into their working environment.

They would learn something new every day and stress and pressure would become part of their daily routine. We had a game plan that would rely heavily on initiative, ingenuity and adaptability, but I was not as confident as I may have appeared. It seemed to me then the phrase 'chasing the dragon' was appropriate to the task before us. The real 'dragons' in this equation were the men who plied their evil trade among the young people of our society. They were vicious, ruthless and determined. I just hoped we were equipped to do more than simply 'chase' them.

4

I decided that a supervising officer would be present on all drug raids and was determined to be present myself whenever possible. We would inevitably be the subject of many allegations and I made it my business to witness personally as much activity as I could.

It was my intention to lead from the front. Being busy with the 'foot soldiers' meant I wasn't at my desk and I was frequently unavailable to some senior officers. My priority, though, was the squad and as I, too, was new to the drug scene, I would learn quicker if I was in the middle of things. In any case, I've always believed that a true copper is the one feeling collars.

Our first bust followed just a few days later and it came as something of a culture shock to see how these people lived. Terry Barnes had been watching a house near Breck Road in Wallasey.

Converted into two flats, only the first floor was occupied and Terry had confirmed that an excessive number of callers stayed for only a few minutes. Late evening was the busiest time and just before 9pm I made my way with Terry, Arthur and the rest of the team to Wallasey.

We arrived laden down with kit-bags and sledgehammers and Terry decided we should go in straight away. By moving in early we could occupy the flat and arrest callers as they arrived. The front door practically opened by itself and we slowly made our way up the darkened stairs. Once outside the flat door, Terry wasted no time. He gave out a roar and smashed a slegehammer into the woodwork. The door burst open and we were met by two petrified women. A baby's cries came from one of the bedrooms, but any sympathy I might have felt for the women evaporated when I saw the obvious signs of drug abuse and dealing: mirror, blades, foils and small quantities of heroin already wrapped into £10 and £5 deals.

Both women were formally arrested and we were told that the male occupant was out dealing but expected back at any time. Some temporary repairs were made to the door-frame and we quietly waited. I covered the door with Arthur while the search team went about their business.

About thirty minutes later we heard footsteps coming up the stairs and readied ourselves as a key was inserted into the lock. Arthur snatched the door open and we both grabbed at the tall, rangy-looking man who stood before us. If he was startled by our sudden appearance, he quickly recovered and ducked beneath our outstretched arms, bolting for the stairs.

We tackled him immediately, but our shouts of "Police!" only ignited a fury of swinging fists and feet. I could hear the footseps of others coming to our assistance when the man made a last desperate lunge to escape. The three of us fell down the stairs locked together and we landed in a heap amid flailing arms and curses. Fortunately, our fall was broken by the suspect and he was quickly arrested. Putting him into handcuffs, Arthur gave me a considered smile.

"I'll tell you what, Boss," he said, "you'll do for me!"

A few days later we followed up a lead developed by Sergeant Derek East, who had replaced Elly Davies a short while earlier; it had always been the intention that Elly would only be with us for a short time pending another posting. Derek had been told that a flat in a high-rise block in Fell Street, Wallasey was being used for supply. The general practice was, and still is, for a raid to be led by the officer responsible for it taking place and Derek, a dependable and efficient member of the squad, had us outside the block at eight in the morning. His information was that a delivery of several ounces of heroin was regularly made there before being distributed to other flats in the area for dealing.

The flat was located on the first floor, but the block was protected by a locked communal door on the ground floor.

To gain entry the lock had to be released by one of the occupants, but if enough bells were rung someone usually released the lock without asking questions.

The target had devised an ingenious system for vetting his callers. The flat next door was un-occupied and he had rigged the wiring so that the bell would ring in his flat. This was only known to *bona fide* callers, so if his own bell rang he was on his guard. That he went to so much trouble only reinforced our suspicions.

His name had come up on our intelligence index and we had little doubt that he was 'at it'. Derek believed the delivery was due at eleven o'clock, but shortly after our arrival we pressed a few buttons and gained access to the block. Once in position, we pressed the bell for the flat next door and, good as gold, the door opened. The man was arrested and we settled down to await the courier.

At precisely eleven, the bell rang. Arthur, in the company of Dave Owens, was allocated the task of dashing down the stairs. They were quickly on their feet and through the door. A few seconds later, I heard screams and raised voices and went down to see what was going on. I was confronted by the sight of Arthur and Dave apologising profusely to a middle-aged woman, visibly shaken. The poor woman, visiting her sister, had been half frightened to death when she had been pounced upon going through the door. Derek joined us and was grace and charm personified.

His soothing words and reassurances soon changed what was a potentially embarrasing situation into a minor distraction. The woman had been mugged only two weeks earlier, but thanks to Derek she agreed that drug abuse was a terrible blight on society and apologised for having got in our way. Derek then pulled me to one side.

"I'm going to have to tell one of the lads to take her home, Boss."

"If you say so, Derek, but isn't she better off sitting with her sister for a while and having a cup of tea?"

"Well, no, not really. She's wet herself." I looked at Derek and we both suppressed a smile. He walked across to Arthur and put a friendly arm around his shoulder.

"Arthur, me old mate, I've got a little job for you."

5

The procedure on a drug raid is unlike any other forced entry operation by police. Drugs can be concealed in the most unlikely places. Cash, too, can be cleverly stashed and great care had to be taken not to miss the smallest nook or cranny. Even the smallest piece of paper might reveal incriminating names or telephone numbers. I wasn't satisfied the current search procedures were adaquate for our purposes, so we developed our own. Ideally, each operation consisted of one detective sergeant and seven detective constables, one at least being female for the purposes of carrying out body searches on women suspects. In this way the thirty-two officer squad was broken down into four teams. On a raid, each officer would be allocated a special responsibility by the officer-in-charge.

One member of the team would be designated

the role of exhibits officer with a responsibility to log all those involved in the search and record every item recovered. He would detail where each item was found and by whom. All evidence was then secured in forensic bags. The suspect would be present throughout the search process and invited to comment as each item was recorded, his answers being noted. Each operation offered excellent opportunities to develop our broader enquiries and could last several hours.

Rooms were searched one at a time with different officers being allocated the floor, ceilings, walls, furniture or fixtures and fittings. Others were detailed to detain callers. The most arrogant of dealers became unnerved as a succesion of customers arrived, each able to reveal damaging information. Many a startled addict walked into our arms when on a routine visit to buy drugs. Basically, the brief of the Wirral Crime Squad was to pursue criminals of all shades, using intelligence gathered from a wide variety of sources and concerning all types of crime. The crimes of dealing, robbery, violence and prostitution were all interrelated. Our main priority was always drug dealing, but we became involved in many other crimes as a consequence.

Raids were often tense and potentially violent occasions and we would often be totally outnumbered. Many addicts at this time would be suffering withdrawal symptoms and the prospect of being locked up and further denied the opportunity to feed their addiction brought out the worst in them.

One officer I perhaps saw more of than any other was Arthur. I'd not worked with him before and overall he was probably the most effective officer I had. Known to the criminal fraternity as 'Mad Dog', he was not particularly tall, but was well-built. I thought him completely fearless and although he didn't give his trust easily, once he did he would follow you over the edge of a cliff. His cheerful, boisterous manner often kept morale high when the going was tough. He was self-motivated, hard-working, completely loyal and frequently a complete pain in the arse.

I'd heard all about him before I ever saw him. He'd had one short stint in the CID before his demented inspector sent him back to his section. When the news got around that Arthur was on board, I received several sympathetic shakes of the head. He was certainly unorthodox and his unconventional methods sometimes needed to be tidied up afterwards, but I succeeded in establishing a very effective relationship with him and I was glad to have him around. I found him impossible to dislike.

One of my favourite remarks when defending Arthur was to say "every squad needs a DC Cowley ... but only one!" It served me right when I was sent another one. Ben O'Brien, a jovial

Irish lad, and Arthur were good friends and the pair of them took turns to torment me. To them I attribute all my grey hair. For all this, they were both excellent police officers and the number of suspects they brought in on charges that turned into convictions was impressive by anybody's standards.

Ben, too, was not unduly fond of his senior officers. He once returned to the station late one evening with his partner Paddy Mahoney and their sergeant, Peter Jones. Peter, a keen rugby player, told them to order the drinks at the bar while he went to the toilet. At the bar, the duty superintendent, who happened to be Jim Heaney, confronted them and gave them a terrific rollocking for drinking on duty. When Peter arrived it was still going on. Ben had a full pint in each hand, one of which was for Peter.

"What's the problem, Sir?" Peter asked.

"The problem, Sergeant, is your two officers here are drinking on duty!"

"Disgraceful, Sir."

"Exactly! Disgraceful! It demonstrates a complete disregard for regulations and an obvious indifference to their responsibilities!"

"I totally agree, Sir." Both Ben and Paddy were glaring hard at Peter, but he didn't bat an eyelid. "Well? What do the pair of you have to say to the superintendent?" Ben attempted to splutter a response.

"I . . . I . . . I'm very sorry, Sir. It won't happen again."

"You're damn right it won't happen again!" The superintendant turned to Peter. "I take it I can leave you to deal with this, Sergeant?"

"Indeed you can, Sir. I take a very dim view of this kind of thing." Once he'd gone, Peter was not the station's most popular DS.

"Well, thanks very much," said Ben.

"What did you expect me to do? You were already in the shit, there was no point in me climbing in with you!"

"Yeah, sure." Ben answered, not yet seeing the funny side, "Here's your pint, Serge!" When Ben told me about it later, I was less than sympathetic.

"It's the sign of a good sergeant who can think on his feet!"

More addresses were raided and arrests made. The squad was getting its feet wet and quickly settling in as an efficient operational unit. They were putting themselves about the division and making their presence felt. The people of the Wirral, especially those living off the fruits of their dealing, knew there were 'new kids on the block'. I was pleased that a healthy number of those arrested were not just addicts but actively involved in dealing.

6

Different talents were emerging among the squad members, not least of which was the ability to wield a sledgehammer. Some took to it as if born for the purpose and a friendly rivalry developed as to who was the best. On sizing up a particular door, one of the lads would propose to smash it within a specified number of blows along the lines of Tom O'Connor's popular TV show *Name That Tune*. The number of proposed strikes would decrease until the whispered chorus went up: "Do That Door!" Success or failure was inevitably settled at the bar afterwards. It was childish stuff, but harmless and good for morale.

On one raid, Jimmy Forrest had impetuously offered to 'do that door in one!' The target was a tenth-floor flat in Lynmouth Gardens in Birkenhead and he'd set himself up on the narrow landing outside the door. He swung the sledgehammer in a wide arc over his head and prepared to bring it crashing down on the door. Unfortunately, as the the hammer reached its peak, the head flew off and disappeared over the parapet. We all watched, hypnotised, as it plummeted more than a hundred feet to the ground below. It landed with a terrific crash but, thank God, hit no one on what was usually a very busy footpath. We later stood around the great hole and admired the damage, mindful of the paperwork had somebody been unlucky enough to have been standing there. It would certainly have put an alternative interpretation on the tabloid headline: Police crash down on drug-dealers!

The loss of a sledgehammer was a blow to the squad as it was one of only two we possessed at the time. Given that as many as four raids might be taking place at any given time, we frequently had to arrange quick visits to local garages, factories or building sites to borrow what we needed. I confess that on occasions tools were taken on a more permanent basis than was the lender's intention.

After we'd been knocking doors down for a month or so I was horrified to receive a bill of £300 for repairs to council property. My mind boggled at what the total cost would come to and I had to act quickly before our wings were clipped and an end was put to forced entry. We enjoyed the active support of the staff of the local council and over a period of time developed effective relationships with many of them. I made a hasty call to one of my contacts and was told to throw the invoice away. Thankfully, I never received another one.

As the months passed, I was constantly surprised at what people were prepared to do for us. Many allowed us into their homes to watch nearby flats and houses and supplied us with coffee, tea and sandwiches no matter how long we stayed. Most people agreed it was a community problem and everybody's responsibiltiy to address it. I know of many people who were rightly proud of the part they played in the downfall of a local dealer.

We were making real progress when the local evening paper, *The Liverpool Echo*, decided to run an expose on the spiralling Wirral drug scene. It included an insight into an industry with a turnover they alleged to be excess of £7,000,000 a year and singled out the police for having been largely ineffective in dealing with it. The report focused entirely on the Wirral, even though the main source of supply was in Liverpool. Much of the content was valid and in a different context we would have welcomed the publicity. From the point of view of my squad, though, the timing was unfortunate. The Wirral Crime Squad wasn't mentioned by name and I doubt if they knew of our existence. We suffered a sharp decline in the information and assistance we received from the public in the weeks that followed.

The article suggested that upward of a thousand addicts were living in Birkenhead and the surrounding areas and highlighted the crisis across the social spectrum. It also included assertions from local solicitors that court cases were being lost due to the poor preparation of prosecution files by police. I was determined that no such claim could be levelled at us. The series ran all week and did us no favours but, to be fair, our successes were fully reported once they became more apparent.

About this time, I attended a Community Forum in Gautby Road Community Hall on the north end estate of Birkenhead with Richard. I was keen to attend. Since our formation, much of the progress we had made was due to the help of local people. Although the general subject of debate was local policing, the entire evening became a heated debate about drug dealing. There were angry and frustrated exchanges and one name was mentioned more than any other: James Miller.

Richard had asked me if I knew Miller when I called him to accept the posting and I had certainly heard of him. He was a large, bull of a man in his early thirties and had developed a reputation for violence on the doors of Birkenhead's night clubs. Having acquired the swagger of the successful criminal, he would go out of his way to taunt police officers as he toured his 'territory'. He was reputed to be the major drug dealer on the Wirral.

Rumour and provable fact are two different animals and although we had no doubt that Miller was a major player, we had no evidence that had the remotest hope of standing up in court. It was suggested on the night that some police officers might be in Miller's pocket. I knew this was nonsense, but he did seem to enjoy a charmed life.

He was unemployed, with no visible, independent means of support, and yet he readily flaunted his affluent lifestyle. He had grown up with one of my lads, Billy Morris, who had an excellent chain of informants. He must have known of Billy's interest in him, but he would openly boast he was untouchable.

He had been a subject of enquiry by the Central Drug Squad for some time and I genuinely believed it was the frustration caused by their lack of success that had motivated Richard into forming the squad. Miller was always our 'most wanted' and Richard badly wanted to see him brought down. We knew there were others above him, but at that early stage I never considered it likely we could penetrate the network beyond him.

7

As the weeks unfolded, we were able to establish the identity of those in control of specific areas and a recognisable network was beginning to emerge. The entire operation seemed to be under the control of one man and we were now convinced that man to be Miller.

Dave Ackerley and his team had been watching a flat in Hillview Heights, Moreton. We knew this neck of the woods to be controlled by Martin Andrews, a well-known face with a string of convictions for violence. Dave, along with Charlie Roughley, had spent a great deal of time on this investigation and was now ready to strike.

Information had been received that the flat was used as a pick-up point for local dealers. Many of the people seen visiting the flat were known addict–dealers. The bust took place early in the evening when the traffic seemed heaviest. Three

men and a woman were arrested. In the subsequent search only a small quantity of heroin was
uncovered but in the next two hours more than
thirty callers had been arrested. It didn't make
sense.

The flat was becoming very congested and
tensions were running high as detained addicts
were suffering from the early symptoms of withdrawal. They were obviously there to be supplied,
but there was no sign of any drugs. Then, quite
dramatically, everything fell into place when the
female occupant of the flat collapsed.

Though barely conscious, she was able to tell
us she had consumed a large quantity of heroin
as we were forcing our entry. She was quickly
removed to hospital where, very luckily, she
later recovered. Tongues were now considerably
loosened and within a short while the main parties
had confessed to a trade in excess of £1,000 a
week. All were later charged and received long
custodial sentences.

This had been our biggest success to date and
I was well aware the news would reverberate
around the drug community. Certainly, we would
have come to the attention of Andrews. He
would have been told all about the raid while
we were still on the premises. This raid was a
notable success right down to the way it proceeded through the courts. We had taken out a
supplier and several small-time dealers in one

swoop. More arrests followed and a couple of days later we were lined up outside a flat in Fender Heights, once again in Moreton. Andrews was certainly having his tail pulled.

Inside the flat a man was arrested but only a small amount of heroin was discovered. Our main target at the address arrived shortly and both men were taken to Wallasey Police Station.

Skilful interview techniques made the most of the information we held. To begin with, the occupant admitted to dealing more than £3,000 worth of heroin a week and confronted with this confession the supplier folded.

He took Dave and his officers to a stash in Ditton Lane, less than a mile away, and admitted since the beginning of the summer to supplying more than £250,000 worth of heroin to a number of local dealers in the network. The drugs recovered in Ditton Lane had a street value of more than £10,000, which at that time represented the biggest haul recovered on the Wirral.

It was also the largest amount a supplier had ever confessed to handling.

This success cost me a small fortune at the bar of Wallasey 'nick', but I was jubilant. We had been in circulation for just a couple of months and had already taken a major supplier out of circulation. Richard, too, was delighted. The arrests were heavily reported in the press and it did much to redress the recent adverse publicity. It was the perfect response.

With Richard I never had anything but a positive and productive relationship. He did, however, possess one irksome idiosyncrasy. He would cheerfully sign and authorise any reasonable claim for incidental expenses, but would watch for accrued overtime like a hawk. He rarely questioned petrol allowance mileage sheets and yet would refuse some modest claims for overtime.

I was once in the interview room at Wallasey with an important suspect when a note was pushed under the door. It was a request to call Richard. I carried on with the interview, but a few minutes later a further note appeared, this time ordering me to ring Richard as a matter of urgency. I stopped the interview, apologising to both the solicitor present and his client. Making straight for a telephone, I asked for Richard's extension. I'd seen him only a couple of hours earlier and I was curious to know what had come up.

"Good afternoon, Sir. It's Mike Mulloy."

"Ah, yes, Mike, thank you for calling me. I'm just working through your squad's submissions for last week's overtime."

"Overtime, sir?"

"Yes, Mike, they seem a little excessive. I really can't accept them."

That was Richard. Conversely, his deputy by

this time was Larry Scullin who didn't object to any amount of genuine overtime, but was a stickler for minimizing expenses. Subsequently, I submitted all the squad's expenses to Richard and the overtime went to Larry. With Molly's collaboration, this worked a treat until the day she was away from her desk for a few minutes. One of the office girls, trying to help, saw the two piles of paper and was aware that Richard and Larry received one each. Unfortunately, Richard got the overtime and Larry got the expenses. The pair of them were on my case for weeks.

8

As the busts continued, so our targets devised ways of increasing their security. A local man, who we were to come across later, was being employed to fix security bolts and grills to the doors and windows of private flats and houses. Today, the technical equipment available to the police would easily overcome this problem, but back in the mid-eighties our most sophisticated weapon was the sledgehammer. The newly installed defences certainly put an end to the cry "I'll do that door in one!"

Dave Gregson and his partner Jimmy Forrest had been watching a flat in Lynmouth Gardens and observed all the classical signs of drug activity. One notable difference was that callers were not permitted to enter the flat, but instead made to exchange cash for drugs through the letter-box. This was a new manoeuvre and again demonstrated how local dealers were responding to our activities.

Late in the afternoon I joined Dave and Jimmy with the rest of the team and we readied ourselves for the bust, confident that sooner or later the door would have to be opened. The landing was more or less deserted and access could be made by either the lift or the staircase. One particular ruse of callers was to take the lift to the floor above and walk down one flight, although most of them avoided the lift altogether. Any police presence could be better 'sussed' from the staircase, but they probably feared mugging more than arrest.

We made our way up the stairs and obtained a clear view of the flat from the stairwell. Other officers were positioned above and below. While we waited a number of callers were intercepted, including a man wanted for burglary, another for handling stolen goods, a youth found carrying a Stanley knife and a woman in possession of a couple of 'snorts' of heroin.

After a couple of tedious hours on the stairs, we were numb with boredom and fatigue. I was about to suggest the lads take turns finding a bite to eat when we heard the bolts being drawn. A young couple appeared and embraced on the doorstep. The mood was shattered when Jimmy leaped forward and slammed into the door with his boot. The couple were detained as the rest of the team quickly entered the flat. We weren't disappointed.

As well as the expected cash and drugs, we arrested more than a dozen callers over the next hour. Every few minutes a gentle tap on the door was followed by a brief conversation through the letter-box. A five or ten-pound note was then pushed through, after which the door was flung open and the startled customer hauled inside.

In addition to the young couple, a third occupant of the flat was arrested and he admitted to a serious level of dealing. Most relevant to our broader investigations was his giving the name of James Miller as his employer. This was the first time Miller had been directly linked to our enquiries by a known associate. It was nowhere near enough to bring him in, but it was the kind of development we had been looking for.

There had been a dramatic rise in the number of search warrant applications and the level of street patrols had been substantially increased. More young people were being stopped in the street and found to be in possession of drugs. To develop public support, it was vital something was being seen to be done.

We sometimes parked our vehicles prominently outside one of the local stations when we were, in fact, several miles away knocking doors over. Word spread and we were effectively able to restrict dealing in more than one area at the same time. We needed to give the impression we were everywhere.

We were making our own luck, but getting the rub of the green also. This was well illustrated when we were waiting quietly outside a flat in Lucerne Gardens on the Woodchurch and were interrupted by a neighbour taking a breath of fresh air. He immediately started to hammer on the target's door.

"Drug Squad! Billy! The Drug Squad!" Incredibly, the occupant took the panic as a wind-up and totally ignored his friend's warning. As we rushed the door, he opened it with a big grin on his face. It soon disappeared and once we were inside we found large amounts of heroin. Within an hour we had another dealer in the cells. Our priority was always heroin, but we did not object to the occasional major cannabis dealer. One such man lived in Wallasey and had been known to the Drug Squad for some time. Steve Quayle got word that he was expected to make a large delivery to another dealer the following day. In this instance, we had to be careful to protect the identity of the informant as, apart from the two targets, he was the only person who knew of their movements.

The following day, Steve and Richie Penston came into work in full uniform and borrowed a marked police car. We followed the two men and at a given signal Steve appeared and pulled them over as if part of a routine stop. The cannabis was then discovered by 'accident'. It worked perfectly and more than a pound of the drug was recovered and a search of the dealer's home uncovered more. To this day, I'm sure he believes he was the unluckiest man in the world to be caught.

9

The general public nearly always referred to us as the Drug Squad, which we were not. We were totally independent of each other, but naturally our paths frequently crossed. Sergeant Alan Jones was a member of the Drug Squad who never lost sight of our common goal.

Both squads had developed an interest in an address off Manor Drive in Upton, the location of which belied its involvement in the business of illegal drugs. One of our teams was to make a move on the man the following morning and because of the Drug Squad's interest, Alan was to lead the raid. The house was actually owned by an elderly couple, but we believed their son, well into his thirties, was allowing a dealer to use the house to store, cut and package his merchandise.

I was expected at the Crown Court that

morning and the raid was due to take place at eight o'clock. However, when I called in at the station just before nine, I was irritated to find the team still there. Alan, not known for his punctuality at that time of the morning, hadn't arrived. When he came dashing in a few minutes later full of apologies and excuses, I admit my manner was brusque.

When they finally got to Upton, the dealer's car was already parked outside the house. Still, if Alan is slow to get his day started, he soon gathers momentum. Rather than ponder and hesitate, he ordered the team to move in straight away. With Mike Parkinson, Peter Challinor and Dougie Brown he led them around the back of the property and in through the kitchen door. Upstairs they caught both men weighing and cutting large quantities of heroin. They were all smiles when they got back.

I was pleased that Alan had redeemed himself as I genuinely liked him. When I heard the commotion of their return, I left my desk and went out to greet them.

"Am I forgiven then, Sir?" Alan asked, full of the exuberance of success.

"Don't ask me, Alan," I answered, giving him a smile that assured him normal service had been resumed, "ask the lads when you buy them that drink you owe them."

Greg Hunt and Steve Longrigg had been

using a flat in Chapelhill Road, Moreton to watch the movements of a man using hire-cars to camouflage his movements. My in-laws, Bill and Elsie Casey, lived close by in Stavordale Road, and in the company of Terry Barnes and his partner, Kenny Gilmour, I paid them a call, being close to the action but out of sight.

Half way through a cup of coffee, the radio crackled into life and Greg told us the suspect had left his flat and disappeared around the back of the building. We quickly went out and were in time to see an unfamiliar car move off in the direction of Birkenhead. We couldn't see the driver but radioed the number-plate through to the control room. It came back as belonging to a local hire-firm. We passed the car as it approached a junction, flagged the driver over and blocked him in. To our surprise, he wasn't our man and nobody recognised him.

Clearly unsettled by our presence, his accent revealed him to be from out of town. He gave no plausible reason for being in Moreton and when his car was searched a large quantity of heroin was found in the boot. He was taken to Upton Police Station where he admitted to regular visits collecting drugs. He used his own car to drive up from Stoke, but would use hire-cars to move around Birkenhead, an idea he had picked up from our original target. We recovered some very interesting documents from the car and were soon able to arrest our local dealer.

10

Back in my office I was generally at peace with the world when I received a call from a most irate Richard.

"Mike, you remember that request from Granada Television a couple of weeks ago?"

"Yes, Sir," I replied, "they wanted to follow us around and film a few busts."

"Right. You know I turned them down?"

"I was glad you did, Sir. We were too busy." I tried to lighten the mood. "I was never one for the smell of the crowd and the roar of the greasepaint!"

"Yes, well, I might have sent them away, but they didn't go away."

"What do you mean?"

"They made their own way down to the Ford Estate and put a programme together. They've filmed deals taking place on the street and the overall tone is that the police are powerless to do anything about it."

"You know that's not the case."

"I know it's not the case and I'd be happier if ten million viewers thought so, too! It's due out in a fortnight and I want it stopped!"

"Stopped?"

"A young man openly bought heroin in front of their cameras. They challenged his assertion that drugs were readily available and within five minutes he'd found a dealer. I want you to find that man and bring him in."

Once again, we seemed destined to take one step forward only to be forced two steps back by the media. I shared Richard's irritation. I called in Arthur, Ben and Les Leddington, one of the squad's female officers, and we made our way directly to the Ford Estate. The TV film was not available to us so we had no idea who we were looking for. Instead, we called in every favour that was owed to us and a few that were not. By eight o'clock that night we had a name and by midnight he was arrested. The 20-year-old was pulled from his bed and before dawn had admitted his part in the film. They were also prepared to name the dealer and he was later brought in.

In the morning Richard rang the programme producer to tell him the film was now sub-judice and could not be broadcast. He added it was also required by the prosecution counsel as evidence.

As this piece of the story was no doubt the part upon which the whole programme would revolve, the plug was pulled and we never heard anymore about it. Richard was well satisfied.

Les Leddington was a lively member of the squad and nothing seemed to get her down. A few days previously, she had been with some of the lads in a police car when they interrupted a street deal going down in the north end. Sitting in the front passenger seat, she jumped out and chased the dealer down the main road. The car followed to give assistance, but instead of passing Les, cruised alongside her. As she glanced across, she saw three grinning males admiring her form as she ran flat out in tight jeans and a close-fitting T-shirt. She let them have the necessary expletives, but took it in good sport. She was always able to give as good as she got.

Many people were surprised at the willingness of arrested dealers and addicts to talk to us. In fact, many 'smackheads' despised the men who exploited their addiction for profit. Those involved in the trade purely for money were known as 'breadheads' and commanded respect by terror. Those with loose tongues could expect the rough justice of iron bars, baseball bats, knives and firearms, but once safely in custody addicts were frequently prepared to tell us all they knew.

Such was the reliability of their information, I

was able to reduce the amount of time spent on unpopular and expensive long-term observations. I was not, though, keen to use their testimony in court. I brought this up with Peter Clarke, head of the local Crown Prosecution Service, and Barney Berkson, a prominent Wirral solicitor who defended many drug addicts in court but who has since sadly passed away. We met at a social function one evening in the town centre and although I was with Carol, conversation soon turned to our 'day jobs'. I mentioned that if ever I were to achieve the level of convictions I was after, I needed witnesses.

"Unfortunately," I told them, "most of the witnesses are smackheads."

"Why don't you use them?" Peter asked. "They can tell the truth like anyone else."

"I agree," Barney said, "as long as no deals are struck to suggest an ulterior motive."

"That's right," Peter added, "if we can convince a jury they have nothing to gain except some consideration from the judge at sentencing, why not?" Hearing this from men on opposite sides of the bench and both qualified to comment, I promised to give it careful consideration.

When I put it to my sergeants and senior constables the next day, there was a general agreement it was worth trying. My initial reluctance had been fostered by my involvement with the 'Supergrass' characters of the seventies.

Vicious criminals had been given exceptionally light sentences in return for incriminating evidence on their associates. The practice had been viewed by some with suspicion and I was not at first prepared to concede our circumstances were very much different. The fact was they were.

Many of the young people we picked up would not have been criminals but for their addiction. Even those dealing at the lower levels did so as an alternative to burglary or shoplifting. I never forgot the distress that they people caused to the public, but many were not habitual criminals until they became involved in drug abuse. For some, their arrest was the first time they had seen the inside of a prison cell. I decided to go ahead. To reduce the potential for allegations of coercion, the arresting officers were not to be involved with potential witness unless myself or a sergeant were present. I insisted on suspects having legal representation at all times. Information received from outside these strict parameters would be acted upon, but not used in court. Whether this policy would help or hinder our level of prosecutions, only time would tell.

11

The walls of my office were by now covered with flow charts and photographs. We had collated intelligence to such a degree over the weeks that I had a clear picture of the network that serviced the Wirral. If my initial instinct that such a structured organisation existed had been verified, I was still surprised as to the extent the peninsular had been purposely and ruthlessly exploited. This fact was consistently confirmed by arrested addicts and dealers. The was nothing co-incidental or accidental about what had happened on the Wirral.

At the head of the network was Peter Burley from Kirkby, a post-war new town just to the north of the Liverpool city boundary. Burley was a huge, intimidating man of formidable appearance. When he made one of his rare appearances on the Wirral he travelled among a flotilla of expensive cars and always in the company of his long-serving minder, Richard Newman, an ex-professional boxer.

Burley, known locally as 'Big Pete', was a shrewd, intelligent man, with the ability to organise his illicit ventures with guile and cunning. He had previous convictions for armed robbery and his reputation ensured he faced no opposition from like-minded criminals in the region. Any interference to the smooth running of what he referred to as the 'Company' was met with swift and vicious retribution. He was used to getting his own way. Of course, above Burley the network spread still further. Criminal financiers had selected him to operate their business on Merseyside and supplied him with all the drugs he could dispose of. These men had distanced themselves from the trade and as we traced Burley's movements, it was clear he was beginning to do the same. I considered it unlikely we would ever get to him. He was meticulous in his planning and evidence that mattered in court would be very difficult to come by. The only real proof of his activities was the testimony of those who worked for him and they would have been in mortal danger had they ever been prepared to stand against him on trial.

Around 1980, Burley had recognised that the Wirral was ripe for exploitation. There was little organisation in place and what illegal drugs were available were supplied from numerous sources. His problem lay in having no connections in the area. Paul McLoughlin was a known addict and petty criminal whose regular visits to Liverpool to purchase heroin demonstrated to Burley an absence of contolled supply on this side of the river.

McLoughlin's address was not known to Burley, so in the company of Newman, he travelled to the Ford Estate and made enquiries. It didn't take long to find him. He was recruited to find persons capable of setting up local drug rings, knowing exactly the kind of people Burley was looking for. In no time at all he had introduced him to James Miller from the Woodchurch, Martin Andrews from Moreton and Gerard Brown, another local hard-man, from the Ford. They would operate within their own areas and recruit dealers to distribute and sell the drugs. Significantly, Miller, Andrews and Brown were not addicts. Most of those they recruited were. Burley was careful who he gave responsibilty to and once McLoughlin had served his purpose the promises of big money and free heroin were withdrawn.

After areas had been designated only one estate was left untouched. Leasowe was in the control of a notorious family and they made it clear they wanted nothing to do with drugs. Though Burley knew he could take Leasowe if he so desired, he wisely decided the effort required and the attention it would draw were not worth it. Other pockets of resistance and those dealers attempting to supply independently were swept away.

Burley had his organisation in place; areas were syndicated, deliveries guaranteed, couriers and dealers recruited and prices established. All he needed now were customers and in finding them Burley and his associates were unforgiveably at their most ruthless. The territory was ideal for their purpose with high unemployment, dissatisfaction and boredom rife among the young. As in the high-rise flats, greater numbers were living outside the restrictions of parental control.

Burley set out to mercilessly exploit the favourable conditions and made a financial investment assured of a rapid and long-term return. In those early days, heroin was given away free with the blatant lie that it was not addictive if the substance was inhaled rather than injected. The free heroin was then withdrawn. This was a major business venture and goes a long way to explaining why the Wirral suffered such a explosion in drug abuse; it was resolutely and carefully nurtured.

I never witnessed nor felt more keenly the despair that heroin brought than on the occasion I was called to a flat were a young woman had been found dead from a heroin overdose. For the sake of her family and her memory, I will give no indication as to where she lived, but before she died she left behind a poem.

It is the the story of a young woman who should have had much to look forward to, but instead was so utterly and completely in despair she decided death was preferable to the life she endured. The poem represents the last thoughts of a woman who still had the clarity of thought to understand the personal cost of her addiction.

Counting the cost of the things I have lost,
The times and the places, the friendships
   and faces,
Hot and then cold, seem to look old,
Is it time to stop?

Crying and shaking, body still aching,
Mind still spinning, must stop grinning,
Vision is blurring, patience is wearing,
Must be time to stop.

Living my life on the edge of a knife,
Loved ones part and cold is my heart,
The end is so near, to die and be clear,
Time to stop.

Trouble and debt, caught in a net,
I've made a mistake, my life I should take,
As a last thing to say, "From smack stay away,"
I wish I could stop.

She was just nineteen.

I was often intrigued by how young people were still attracted to heroin long after its evil reputation became established. I found it incredible that so many continued to succumb to its fatal attraction. Once addicted they seemed to have no will to be rid of it. I asked one arrested young woman what she got from it all.

"Now?" she asked and I nodded. "If I want to feel as normal as you do when you wake up every morning . . . I have to take smack."

It was a chilling thought.

12

It was approaching Christmas when we received information regarding Burley that was to alter my view that he could not be caught. Dave and Jimmy had been preparing to hit two flats in Ford Towers on the Ford Estate. When they were taken, we were initially disappointed. There was only a small quantity of heroin on the premises and the two dealers we had expected to pick up were out. The team was stood down and I arranged that we should meet up at Wallasey Station.

We were on one of the upper floors of the block and waiting for the lift. As usual, most of the lights had been smashed and it was quite dark. When the lift arrived the doors opened and revealed the presence of Ged Allen, a known addict and small-time dealer. He stepped out in front of us but immediately shrank back in horror and cowered, with his arms raised over his head, begging not to be beaten. I had no idea what he was going on about, but both Dave and Jimmy knew him well and entered the lift before the doors closed. When he realised he'd stumbled into the company of police officers, his relief overwhelmed him.

"Oh, Jesus! I thought it was them! I thought you was them! They're gonna kill me! They're gonna fuckin' kill me! I'm a dead man! Oh, thank God it's you!" For someone who would never have been far from the top of our list of people to talk to, he was surprisingly pleased to see us. We didn't so much escort him to our car as try to keep up with him. He was taken to Upton and the lyrics to his song were pure gold. He told us he had been acting as a courier to James Miller, making regular excursions to Liverpool to collect large quantities of heroin. This was a missing link in our flow charts. We knew that Miller and Burley were no longer making regular trips across the river and had correctly assumed they were using couriers. Now we had one. Allen had been dealing directly with Burley and was able to tell us where he lived. He went on to confess he had allowed Miller to use his flat for regular meetings with his distributors and dealers.

He had personally witnessed Miller dealing and confirmed that he was the top man on the Wirral, senior to Brown and Andrews in the network.

"You must know that," he insisted. "Shit! Everyone knows that!" He then went on to tell us why he had been so relieved to be taken into custody. A few weeks earlier, Miller had taken his family to the United States and had a friend of his, John Wescott, handle the business while he was away. We knew Westcott and knew the only real qualification he had for the job was loyalty; he could be trusted.

Allen had been over to Liverpool and collected Miller's usual consignment of heroin. On his return he decided to make the most of Miller's absence and take a small amount of the package for himself. He clearly didn't anticipate that Wescott, whom he neither feared nor respected, would hear of it. He then cut the deals, each fractionally light to compensate for what he had taken, and passed them on to the dealers. It was a stupid and dangerous mistake, but Allen was a chronic addict, not known for his clarity of thought.

As in most business operations, customers check their deliveries. Word came back from a number of dealers that the packages were light and Burley blew a fuse. His credibility was vital to the smooth running of his network and Burley neither desired nor could afford to let the discrepancy pass. When Miller returned, they went to Allen's flat in Upton late one evening. While Burley waited in his Mercedes, Miller dragged a pleading Allen from his flat. He was thrown into the back of the car and taken down to the beach at Hoylake. He was beaten and threatened with having his legs broken. Finally, he confessed to stealing from the consignment. He was beaten some more and told to repay the money, after which he was thrown from the car.

A couple of weeks passed and Allen had still not found the money. One evening, his front door was smashed down and four men threatened him with a sawn-off shotgun and demanded the money. The trigger was pulled and the gun clicked. He was shown an unused cartridge.

"Next time this goes in the gun." He screamed that he would repay the money and the men left. He owed Burley for just two grammes of heroine, at that time worth about £140. For this he had beaten and his life threatened.

Unable to stay in his own flat, he had drifted around those of close friends, well aware they would catch up with him sooner or later. In a police station cell, he felt for the first time in several weeks that he might live beyond the next few days. He really had few options left open to him but to co-operate with us.

After a lengthy interview, he was charged and appeared before the Birkenhead Magistrates Court the following morning. He was remanded for three days to a local station where he be could questioned further. Over those few days many of the gaps in our intelligence were filled, many of the things we suspected were confirmed and many men we knew to be offenders could now be arrested. Our guest received the very best of attention and he was one young man who did not complain about the thickness of the walls. Burley and Miller had maintained an empire on the foundations of terror and violence. Ironically, that very policy had driven one of their own number singing into our arms.

Despite the quality and quantity of Allen's information, we had to tread very carefully. Burley and Miller were still at large and while they were, much of the evidence we could build against them was vulnerable. I knew from personal experience that once such men are taken off the streets, birds sing.

We now had a very real chance of taking Burley, one of the biggest dealers in the north of England. It was desperately tempting to move in straight away, but patience was an essential virtue. If we missed him now, we would not get another chance.

Burley would have been aware that Allen had been picked up but probably felt the terror instilled in him would guarantee silence.

It was an uncharacteristic mistake. While Miller was still around, Burley would feel safe. If people further down the chain of command had not been picked up, he would feel we had nothing on him. It was impossible to get to Burley any other way than through Miller. But what if we by-passed

Miller and went for Burley first? Undoubtedly, the best time to arrest a man is when he least expects it. From a psychological point of view and for the impact it has on his organisation, far more is gained when a man is dramatically plucked from his home. The reaction could be such that if Burley was brought in, the rigid discipline that controlled the whole organisation might fall in. Instinctively, self-preservation reigns.

All other activity had to continue as normal, but I brought in Dave Ackerley, Arthur and their team to concentrate on all intelligence gathering regarding Burley. If I'm honest, I probably expected too much from the team in those days, but they were as committed to the goal as I was and morale was exceptionally high. We were taking on the biggest drug cartel known in this part of the country and had little but our enthusiasm to help us. Everyone was excited at the prospects.

Every day we were taking on the dealers, smashing doors in and making arrests. We needed tensions to run high. Those dealers who hadn't yet been picked up were nervous of every sudden movement, living constantly in fear of imminent arrest. Within the squad, there was a distinct pride in what they were doing. I was aware of the increasing number of requests to join the squad, which meant I could carefully vet and select who came on board. Our reputation was spreading within the Force. Everybody was giving everything and it was a pleasure to come into work.

Risley Remand Centre was filled to overspill. The mood was such we heard of many stories attributing to us deeds that were pure fiction. We didn't discourage it. When taking out a tenth-floor flat in Lynmouth Gardens a window was smashed. The word flashed around the Woodchurch that men of the squad had absailed down the outside of the block and smashed their way into the flat through the windows. We heard other tales of unco-operative suspects being thrown off the top of tower blocks.

Even members of the force were guilty of believing the publicity. Each week I had to submit a report to several senior officers up to the rank of detective chief superintendent. We had been asked to accompany officers in Liverpool to a night-club where there had been reported an excessive amount of drug-dealing. Given that we now knew so many faces in the business, it was hoped that we could recognise some of the dealers present. The evening went well from our point of view and several arrests were made. When I included this in my report the following week, one senior officer thought we had taken it upon ourselves to go chasing over to Liverpool and drag our suspects from the club without invitation or clearance.

I was quite happy that the squad was

developing a reputation for being unpredictable, fearless and omnipresent. I don't think many outsiders could make sense of our methods and tactics, but the truth was everything was carefully planned and monitored. The impression of disorder was our creation, but existed only in the minds and lives of the 'dragons' we pursued.

13

Steve Longrigg and Greg Hunt were lined up for a bust in Hoole Road on the Woodchurch and were short of manpower. I'd had a court appearance that morning and on my return decided to join them, taking Arthur and Mike Morgan with me. Arthur complained all the way, asserting the raid would be a complete waste of time. It was typical of Arthur who, because he had so much going on himself, was loath to be distracted with someone else's problems. In contrast, when he was organising a raid himself, he wanted the world and his cousin to be there.

Arthur's sentiments were compounded when we arrived at the address.

"Well, now I know we're wasting our time!"

"Why, Arthur?" Not for the first time, he was wearing me out.

"That house. I've got an informant living there.

She's been giving me bits and pieces for ages. If there was anything going down here, I'd have known about it weeks ago." According to Steve, the house was being used as a store and the dealer, another woman, called regularly to collect drugs as she needed them.

As there was no dealing done from the address, we decided not to force entry but instead walked up to the door and rang the bell. When the door opened, we rushed in and secured the premises in the usual way. Arthur was the last to make an entrance and his continual bleating stopped dramatically when he saw drugs and cutting gear on the coffee table. If this surprised him, he was completely startled by the presence of one of the best known addicts on the estate.

He was furious, both because he now had egg on his face and his informant had been leading him a song and dance. Arthur, though, was the consumate professional. Putting his bruised ego to one side, he sat down with the girl he thought he knew so well and started talking to her.

He somewhat redeemed himself when after a few minutes she led him to the toilet in the rear yard and pointed to an area near the pan. From under the swathes of pipe cladding we retrieved several packages of heroin and cash. Shortly afterwards, we were elated when our raid coincided with a visit from the dealer who we found had more heroin and a great deal of cash in her possession. A further search of her home revealed more. We'd had a little bit of luck but the job had gone well and Steve and Greg were to be applauded for the work they'd put in. They also had the added pleasure of bringing it up if ever they thought Arthur had too much to say.

Terry Barnes and Barry Jones had been following yet another lead in Lynmouth Gardens. It was suggested on more than one occasion that we should set up a mobile incident room outside Lucerne and Lynmouth Gardens on the Woodchurch. I don't think there was a time in the early days when we weren't preparing to carry out a bust there. Mark Clemson once said that on leaving the station one night on his way home, he turned in the direction of Lynmouth Gardens before he realised where he was going.

We were so regular in attendance that the council were usually able to provide us with observation flats at very short notice. In general, I was impressed with the co-operation we received from the council. Their staff went to great lengths to assist us and accommodate our sometimes unusual requests.

The flats we used were sometimes sparsely furnished but to some degree comfortable enough to spend a few hours in. Others were nothing more than rat-holes. Such work could be harrowing for the squad and a great strain. In order that the post was not detected, the flats had to be entered very early and left late. That might mean officers spending as long as sixteen hours in these places without a break. When no bust was anticipated and the nature of the occupation was a watching brief, the tedium was murderous.

On this occasion, with Barry and Terry, we were going to extreme lengths to maintain complete silence. We had been in position since 7am. We knew from our contacts that the flat was heavily guarded with iron bars and grills, so a frontal attack with sledgehammers was a waste of time. The morning dragged on and the team were weary with waiting. It seemed the door would never open.

Suddenly, Terry stiffened and called for silence. We could hear the bolts and locks being drawn back and Terry and Barry went slowly into the corridor. The door finally opened and a young male stepped out. Both the lads were on him in an instant and we quickly followed. Rushing into the flat we could hear desperate attempts were being made to flush something down the toilet. On entering it, we found another man with large quantities of heroin. A violent struggle ensued. He was quickly overpowered and arrested. There were several other people in the flat and while we there a knock on the door was answered and produced another dealer carrying drugs and cash. All were subsequently interviewed and charged with supply.

One unexpected bonus was the presence of the man responsible for the design and installation of the iron-made security systems that were now scattered across the Wirral. He'd caused us no end of problems and taken the art of entering a suspect flats on to a higher plain. He was neither an addict nor a dealer and he was clearly distressed when he read his charge sheet listing a string of conspiracy charges related to the sale of prohibited class-A drugs.

At one flat we knew to be heavily protected, Frank Sherratt knocked on the door in overalls, carrying a clipboard and a boxed video recorder. His knocks were answered by a shout through the door.

"What do you want?"

"Video!"

"What?"

"Video! I'm delivering your new video!"

"What new video? Nobody's ordered a new fuckin' video here!"

"Don't mess me about, mate, I've got another dozen calls to make. It's your address on the invoice. Maybe somebody's bought it for you. Just take the thing off me, will yer? I'm not bothered who ordered it." The door was finally opened and we all pounced. The dealer was clearly annoyed with himself.

"I should have known it was a fuckin' ruse," he said, "Manweb cut me 'lecky' off last week!"

Nobody said you needed brains to push drugs. Our concentration was clearly focused on the Burley/Miller enquiry, but inevitably arrests included many shades of criminal.

We expected nothing else. At the lower end of the drug trade, addicts were involved in a variety of crimes to subsidise their habit. It was because of this that we faced interference from higher authority. The CID wanted the Wirral Crime Squad split into two sections with one half concentrating on drugs and the other on burglaries. Their influence was based on the number of CID officers in the squad and, despite my protestations, the squad was divided into two sections. It was very frustrating, but in fairness to Richard, the prospects must have seemed promising.

We had been more effective than anybody could have expected and I felt that dividing the squad was a retrograde step. An important element of our success came from treating the crimes of theft and drug-abuse as related. Burglars were invariably drug-addicts and they led us to the dealers.

It came as no surprise to me when the detection rate fell. The half of the Squad dealing with burglaries came under the immediate control of a detective inspector from Wallasey. He insisted on plain-clothes officers wearing suits which made them only slightly less conspicuous than if they had been wearing full uniform. It wasn't working and within six weeks Richard had seen enough. We returned to our original shape and, as if to force the point, we quickly restored arrests back to their earlier levels.

We were picking up something like three or four people every day and it was a testimony to our efforts and preparations that very few were pleading not guilty in court. This was actually more important than it seemed at face value. If cases had to be proven it could be costly in terms of manpower as officers were tied up in court giving evidence.

We were given assistance from a variety of sources and on one bust in Moreton were assisted by a three-year-old child. Inside the flat, we had recovered little in the way of hard drugs, but one of my officers, Julie Wallace-Jones, sat down to chat to the young toddler.

"What was Mummy doing before we got here?" she asked.

"She was puttin' bags in the big box in the toilet," she innocently answered. The 'big box' turned out to be the water-cistern and a considerable amount of heroin was recovered. Out of the mouths of babes . . .

A more poignant way in which children became embroiled in drugs was witnessed on one raid when we interrupted a young girl playing with a pair of plastic scissors and a magazine. When she was asked by Steve Littlejohn what she was making, she looked full of youthful innocence.

"I'm playing Mummy's game cutting up drug wraps."

I was driving around the Woodchurch with Terry Barnes and George Kettle one Sunday afternoon and decided to take a look around a block of flats. Quite often, when we had nothing else to follow up at a particular moment, we would enter a block and from the landings shout "Police!" or "Drug Squad!" We never got any arrests this way, but we had the satisfaction of watching plastic bags being flung from windows and hearing the sound of toilets flushing all over the block.

On entering the lift we were met by a known addict who quickly put his hand to his mouth and swallowed hard. He told us he had dropped a quarter gramme of heroin. Apart from that he was clean and there was little we could do with him. We did, however, start chatting and pursuaded him to reveal the name of his supplier. He'd been supplied by two girls and we went straight to the flat where quantities of drugs were found. As it happened they weren't drugs at all but pepper. The two girls had been ripping everybody off, so we charged them with deception. There was a lot of sneezing on the Woodchurch that night.

Christmas was upon us and even on Christmas Day we took our seasonal greetings to the dealers and offered them alternative accommodation. We were Carol Singers and delivery men or whatever it took to get doors open.

We received a Christmas Card from eight dealers on the Woodchurch we'd locked up a few weeks earlier and were spending the hoiliday in Risley Remand Centre. The card read:

> To the Sledgehammer crew
> Merry AXEmas
> From the Woodchurch Boys

At least they held no grudges.

For those of us who had joined the squad back in August, we only had until the end of January before we were returned to our sections, so the Christmas party took on the form of a rehearsal for our imminent parting. In uniform, I had spent the last five Christmas nights on duty and I was happy that this time around I would be with Carol. I was able to spend some time looking back over what had been achieved and looking forward to returning to my office in Birkenhead.

I should have known better.

14

At the beginning of 1985, I was generally pleased with the direction our enquiries were taking. The interview rooms were busy as we built up our case against Burley and Miller. We knew about the chain of command on the Wirral and were finding who worked for each dealer and supplier. All the strings ran back through to Miller and then Burley.

The work was pedantic and difficult, but we were now able confidently evaluate the information we had. As we were getting close to Burley, I was mindful of the fact that he had been the target of the Central Drug Squad for a long time. They were not aware of our progress and I had to be wary of treading on their toes. We had one major advantage over the Drug Squad in this regard; all the people who could provide the testimony that would put Burley away were on the Wirral. We knew far more about them than the Drug Squad.

The fact that we were making serious progress was verified by the rise in tension among the criminal elements. Reports of shootings and mindless acts of violence were filtering back to us. Trust between the factions was disappearing. People inside the network were talking to us and dealers did not know who they could trust.

In considering what intelligence we held, I knew that most of it was nothing but that. Very few of the people who revealed information to us were either prepared to stand up in court or, if they were, could not be trusted. Of those that could, a number would be easily manipulated and would be broken down by a competent defence counsel. I decided it was still too early to be collecting corroborative statements from those I felt could be valuable to us in court. I didn't at this stage want Burley or Miller to know how far we had come.

I was now due to return to my section, but given the critical stage of the investigation I readily agreed with Richard that I and those officers closest to the Burley enquiry should stay on for the time being. At the end of the month, I had members of Ackerley's team concentrating almost exclusively on plotting Burley and Miller's downfall.

At 7.30am on 6th February, Phil Davis and his team took out three addresses in rapid succession on the north end, seizing a substantial haul of heroin. Those arrested were taken to Birkenhead Police Station, two admitting to serious levels of supply. From two of those arrested we learnt that Miller was both fully aware and completely indifferent to our interest in him. Confirmation of this made me think long and hard about just how much longer we should leave it before we moved for him. On the one hand, we had to have the best case possible to take into court and yet the longer we left it the better he could prepare himself and distance himself from the crimes. It was a difficult decision. In the short term, I decided to rattle Miller's arrogant indifference. Every suspect we held was questioned closely about Miller, whether or not there was a known connection. Before long, he was hearing all about our apparent 'obsession' with him.

News of firearms being used in recriminations and revenge attacks were becoming commonplace. As panic gathered momentum, criminals were jostling for position to be best placed when the roof fell in. Some relationships were found to be more than a little fragile, although this struggle was taking place beneath Burley. Whoever emerged the stronger would still be supplied by Burley. We recovered a shotgun from the Ford after arresting two men who admitted that they had spoken of killing another dealer before they themselves were killed. As the tentacles of our operation began to reach out, the facade of unity between the suppliers and dealers was beginning to crumble.

A few days later, I was watching a house in Briardale Road, Birkenhead in the company of Arthur, Paddy, Julie, Mike Craven, Charlie Roughley and John Smith. This was quite close to the town centre and we were there a full three hours before we saw any movement. We had heard the female living in the house was of previous good character, employed full time as an office clerk. Although not an addict, her boyfriend was an associate of Miller and Burley. The boy-friend was a taxi-driver who had made so much money in a short time from drug trafficking he was able to buy his own taxi firm. The girl was believed to be a courier and the house used for storing heroin. At half five, she arrived home. She was an attractive girl aged about 20, called Maria Brooke When she was told of the nature of the call she accepted her fate immediately. A short while later the boyfriend, Paul Sinnot, arrived. Both were taken to the station at Birkenhead while the house was searched. Sinnot's house was also searched.

Brooke told us she had been having an affair with Sinnot, a married man, since August 1984 and that he had been a friend of Miller's for some ten years. Sinnot had told her of his intention to purchase heroin from Miller to raise the money for his own firm and that initially she had only allowed him to use her home as a safe house. Before long she was acting as a courier, meeting with both Burley and Newman to collect drugs on his behalf. She had received little monetary gain and had foolishly done it for love.

Sinnot also made a full confession and confirmed that he had known Miller since 1974. He had resisted Miller's early approaches but had finally succumbed at the possibility of earning so much money. He was a novice but most of his early customers were provided by Miller. He could not give us Burley's address, but knew where Newman lived. He reckoned he had dealt in the region of many thousands of pounds worth of heroin, a figure we now had no difficulty believing, and stressed that Brooke had never been more than a courier and not in Miller's employ. Both were charged and held on remand.

Sinnot and Brooke were prepared to testify in court and give their general demeanour I believed they would both make excellent witnesses, especially as they had direct contact with Burley and Miller. If I moved now I knew we would find nothing at the homes of Burley and Miller, but I could use the time between the arrests and the trial to build up a strong case against them. Once they were inside, reliable informants would be much easier to come across.

I went to see Richard and suggested to him that now was the time to move, but that we should take Burley first. I believed this would have dramatic inpact on the whole network. It had got back to Miller we showing an excessive interest in his activities and the desired affect had been achieved. We were receiving information that Miller was becoming increasingly paranoid. Richard was understandably reticent about taking Burley first. He had always regarded Miller as the main priority and knew he ran the Wirral, Richard's Division. I argued the case that if we took Miller out Burley would have someone in his place within hours.

There was also the issue of the Central Drug Squad. They held a bulging file on Burley but had never collected the evidence to arrest him. Richard, though, was satisfied that if our enquiries led us directly to a suspect outside of our division we were totally justified in applying for a warrant to search his home address. We tussled for a while over the different factors involved but eventually Richard relented.

"I gave you a job to do and you haven't let me down. Do it your way."

I held a conference in the squad room and gave those not directly involved the fine detail. They had worked hard, most of them for over six months, to arrive at this moment. I decided on the date we would go in. There was some surprise but a definite sense of elation and exitement. All hands put their shoulders to the wheel of preparation for the big day. We were going for Burley first.

On the evening of 14th February, the night before going to Kirkby for Burley, I went over to the Woodchurch with Dave and Arthur. Two sisters, Debbie and Sandra Coulton, had been addicts and were familiar with the activities of both Burley and Miller.

I knew that Sandra in particular had developed an intense loathing for the pair. If she was willing, I felt she would make a vital witness for the quality of the evidence she could give. The strength of her personality would enable her to stand up to intense cross-examination. She would prove a valuable asset and I knew I would feel far more confident picking Burley up if she was in our camp.

I spoke to Sandra in the presence of her mother and sister. There was no denying she was taking an enormous risk; she would come under enormous personal pressure once it became known that she was prepared to testify. I was much relieved when she readily agreed. As there could be no suggestion of her 'cutting a deal', she was likely to be our most credible witness. I'd had many dealings with the family in the past and I knew I could trust her. Conversely, she had no reason to trust me. She owed me no favours and my admiration for her knew no bounds.

Just before 11pm, I rang the duty inspector at

the Central Drug Squad to let him know we were going in for Burley the following morning. He was not pleased to hear it but, after a short pause, wished me luck, adding it was about time Burley had some grief in his life. We had stolen their thunder, but the witnesses were on our side of the river and we were ready to go.

I slept little that night.

15

I held a final briefing at the Manor Road station at 7am on the morning of 15th February. We discussed what we had to do and how we would react given a number of hypothetical situations. The mood was tense but expectations were high. At half seven, four cars left the station car park and made their way down Liscard Road towards the Kingsway Mersey Tunnel. The journey to Kirkby took about half-an-hour at that time in the morning. One of the cars went to Walton to keep an eye on Newman's home. We would join them later.

We parked outside Burley's home. Paul Lathom and Ben O'Brien took up a position at the rear of the property, Andy Stewart and Mark Clemson covered the cars and I made the walk up the short path in the company of Dave, Arthur, Paddy and Julie. Dave had led this part of the enquiry, so his team would make the arrest. We had no idea what to expect and apart from his BMW being parked outside, had no confirmation that he was actually at home.

Julie knocked loudly and with authority on the door and a few seconds later the door was opened by Burley himself. I had seen several poor quality photographs of the man, but this was the first time I had met him. I needed no explanation to why he struck fear into the hearts of those who crossed him. He must have been six foot four and some eighteen stone and the violence within him was immediately apparent. Dave introduced us and produced the search warrant, which Burley took and read.

Although a council property, Burley's home was expensively furnished. In the presence of his wife and two sons, Dave told him we intended to search the house, but not surprisingly no drugs were found. We did, though, seize bank account statements and cheque books, bills and address books. When we were finished, Arthur approached Burley.

"Peter Burley, I am arresting you on suspicion of being concerned in conspiracy to supply drugs. You are not obliged to say anything, unless you wish to do so, but whatever you say will be taken down in writing and may be given in evidence." Burley didn't flinch.

"I don't know what you're talking about."

He was placed in Arthur's car and shortly after nine we were outside Newman's home in Walton. In front of his terraced house, Arthur and Paddy waited in the car with their suspect. Arthur watched as we entered the house and turned to Burley.

"Do you know who lives there?"

"No idea."

"Richard Newman?"

"Never heard of him."

"You don't know Richard Newman?"

"No."

Our knock was answered by a man in his early twenties who turned out to be Newman's son and also a boxer. We asked for his father and entered the living room. Newman was lying on the couch and a heavy young man, a friend of his son's, was seated opposite. This was also the first time I had been in the presence of Newman and although I sensed an air of menace about him, he seemed fairly philosophical about our presence. He was told who we were, the reason for our visit and was given the warrant. At this, his son flipped.

"What the fuckin' hell's happening? Who the fuck do you bastards think you are? Fuck off! Go on! Fuck off! Get the fuck out!" The other young man didn't say a word but stood up and I thought we had trouble. The situation was defused by Newman himself.

"Mark, hold your tongue. The officers here are

only doing their job. Let them do it." His son immediately did as he was told and his friend sat down. There was no problem with parental discipline in this household. Newman then looked directly at me.

"Help yourself, lad."

The search of both houses had been low key and I doubt if the neighbours noticed we were in the street. They were both professional criminals and knew they may later regret any resort to violence. Their best ploy was to plead ignorance and let us prove our case against them if we could. Once Newman was in the street, he exchanged glances with Burley, but did not acknowledge him. I'm sure Burley's presence in the back of a police car did nothing to reassure Newman. They were both taken to the Wirral in separate cars.

I was in the front passenger seat of the vehicle escorting Newman. As we left the Mersey Tunnel at Birkenhead, he spoke for the first time.

"How long is this gonna take, Inspector?"

"How long is a piece of string?" I replied.

"I've left me ciggies in the house. Any chance we can stop for some?"

"Have you got any money on you?"

"Yeah."

"I smoke myself. I know what it's like." I told Dave to pull over in Market Street at a newsagents near to the station. Newman passed me a £5 note.

"Get us forty Bensons, Boss." When I got back

into the car I passed him cigarettes and change. He nodded as he took them from me. "You're not bad, Inspector."

The two men were independently searched, booked and lodged in separate cells. Arthur escorted Burley and told him he had to attend court and would see him later.

"What are you after?" Burley asked him.

"You've already been cautioned, Peter, you and another male are the Wirral's main drug suppliers."

"I can give you the other fella on a plate."

"Like I say, Peter, I'm due in court. I'll see you later."

I was engaged in the Crown Court for most of the day, so in the early part of the afternoon, Burley was taken to the Interview Room by Dave and Julie. He was again reminded he had already been cautioned and that he was now to be formally interviewed on tape regarding the supply of drugs.

"I'm not saying anything on tape. I'll talk to you now, but not on tape."

"Alright, Peter, but at the end of the day, it's got to go on tape."

"No way, you tell me what you want and I'll see what I can sort out."

"Alright Peter, Let's put it this way. I have reason to believe you are involved in the major supply of controlled drugs on the Wirral and by that I mean the supply of diamorphine, commonly known as heroin or smack, is that right?"

"You don't expect me to put my head in a noose do you?"

"Look, we know you have been pushing heroin on the Wirral through James Miller."

"Who's he?"

"Peter, don't play games, we've got sightings of you with Miller."

"I don't know him, who are you talking about?"

"Look Peter, I can prove you were a front seat passenger in a car with Miller when he ran down a kid and killed him. Now that's something you wouldn't forget, isn't it?"

"Who says I was in the car?"

"You've got a bad memory when you want Peter. I've got a statement made by you as a witness to the accident, that was November 1983, so don't tell me you don't know him."

"Okay, I was in the car when he killed the kid. So what, that doesn't prove I'm selling heroin, does it?"

"It proves you know him."

"Alright, I've only got to say that we did some business over buying and selling second-hand cars."

"I know you were dealing heroin with him."

"You might know it I was dealing in heroin but can you prove it?"

"Peter, I'll prove it but what I want from you is your part in the heroin trade."

"No chance, if I said what I've been doing, no Judge in the world wouldn't give me less than a ten stretch. You must think I'm soft."

"I've got no control over what a Judge might give you, but I'll stand up in Court and say you've helped us if you do."

"Look, I could take you to the top of the tree, but what's in it for me?"

"Only what I've said, I'll tell the Court that you helped us, that's all."

"You can kiss my arse, you know I've been dealing, I know it, but I want a good deal out of it."

"Look Peter, I can only do what I've already said."

"No chance, I want some guarantees before I help you. I want out without charges. Then I'll tell you the score."

"There can be no guarantee Peter, you've got to tell us the truth about your part, then maybe I can help you at the court with what ever else you can tell us."

"No, I'm wasting my time here. You might as well get my brief before I say anymore if you don't want to deal."

"There are no deals Peter, I'll get your solicitor then I want to interview you on tape."

"Look, there's no way I would say any of this

on tape unless you could guarantee me a walk out."

"I don't think there is any point taking this further, I'll contact your solicitor."

"Think on this, I could stop the supply of heroin on the Wirral which is what you want but I want to walk out, no charges. You know what I mean and some people I could give you are a lot bigger than me, you know what I mean."

"Peter, I want what's in your head. I want the people above you but there's no way I can close my eyes to your involvement in heroin."

"There's no point talking to you then, just get me my brief."

At this point the interview was brought to a close and Burley was returned to his cell.

Later in the day Arthur returned from the court and as the arresting officer went to see Burley to complete the some paper work. As he was doing so, Burley made him an offer.

"If I get a walk out tonight, with no charges, you get a rub down." He held up two fingers. "Two grand."

"Not interested, mate," Arthur told him. He left the cell and immediately reported this offer to supervision. Dave rang Richard who gave permission to have Arthur wired up in an attempt to have the attempted bribery recorded. This involved the attendance of an officer from the

Technical Support Unit, who sealed the tape in such a manner that it could be proved that it had not been tampered with. Burley repeated his offer, but the conversation took place through the cell door and the recording was dreadful. He was street wise enough to know it might have been a trap and was guarded in his choice of words. Much was to be made of this tape at the subsequent trial.

When I returned from the Crown Court I was brought up to date, and with Dave I again interviewed Burley. I cautioned him again and put the fresh allegation to him.

"I have been informed that you have made an offer of £2,000 to Constable Cowley for charges not to be proceeded with."

"Who's Cowley?"

"He is the officer you have just been dealing with." I also informed him that the latter conversation was tape recorded as Arthur had been wired up. Burley shrugged his shoulders.

"Let's see what's on the tapes." I cautioned him again and told him the matter would be the subject of a report. He made no reply.

Even at this early stage, Burley was clearly rattled and this surprised me. He knew the Drug Squad had been chasing him for an age, but he gave the impression he had no idea where the Wirral Crime Squad came into the equation. He remained arrogant, but I could see the anxiety in his eyes. He was clearly surprised at being arrested and caught completely off balance.

The interview with Newman could not have provided a greater contrast. He was reminded he was still under caution and the interview was to be taped. The whole thing took less than a minute.

"You're wasting your time. Nothin' personal, but you might as well put me back in me cell and let me get me head down."

"I've just told you, you don't have to say anything, but I am obliged to ask you some questions about the offence for which you have been arrested."

"Look, you've either got your evidence or you haven't. Charge me or let me go. I've got nothing to say."

"You don't wish to say anything about your involvement in the supply of drugs, namely heroin?"

"I've got nothin' to say."

"Take him back to his cell."

Burley was later formally charged with conspiracy to supply heroin, supplying the same and unlawful possession. Although his solicitor objected, the prosecution successfully remanded him in custody. Newman was released on police bail prior to the holding of identification parades, but was later arrested and also charged with conspiracy to supply.

If Miller was paranoid already, he must have

been in pieces when he received the news of Burley's arrest. He would have known it was impossible for us to have a case against Burley without having more evidence on him. The squad was very busy over the next few days. We had coupled the arrests with an extended spate of activity and we were pulling in dealers from all over the peninsula. Miller, however, had disappeared.

16

Miller was nowhere to be found. We watched his home and his usual haunts, but he had gone to ground. Billy Morris and a detective constable from the Drug Squad, Brendan Farrell, approached me and said they were in touch with an informant who said he could give us Miller. For a few days I put considerable manpower into this line of enquiry, but we were soon having problems. His 'safe house' became a 'flat' and then he 'moved'. We were then told he'd been to London, but was travelling back on the Monday and would be carrying heroin. We were at Lime Street Station long before the first London Euston train pulled in, but there was no sign of Miller. I was less than impressed with the informant. It was a long cold day and eventually I had to stand the lads down. Billy and Brendan suggested bringing the informant in for me to see personally.

I thought that was probably a good idea.

When they brought him in the following day, it turned out to be McLoughlin, the man originally used by Burley to establish the Wirral ringleaders. He suggested that we give him £500 and he would personally use it to buy heroin from Miller. As the exchange was taking place, we were supposed to step in and arrest him. Such practice is completely illegal and I left McLoughlin in no doubt that I would have no part in it.

He did not pursue the point but continued to propose different methods of entrapment which required some illicit behaviour on our part. I could smell a rat and when searched it turned out McLoughlin was wired. Trusting him with such a task was an error on Miller's part for he soon coughed the details. In conjunction with a man I had not come across for a couple of years, Terry Merson, Miller was seeking to obtain evidence that could be used to show malpractice if and whenever he was brought to trial. We were to hear a lot more of Merson before very long, but on this occasion I was pleased that we had both foiled an amateurish effort to embarrass us and had seen how desperate Miller was becoming. McLoughlin was himself later arrested and charged with his part in the supply of heroin.

McLoughlin cut a rather pathetic figure, totally lacking in self-confidence and usually doing his best to ingratiate himself with police officers. On one occasion, I was transferring him from Wallasey to appear at the Birkenhead Magistrates Court in the company of Mark Clemson. As we approached the courts, I was driving down a one-way street and slowed to a stop as a woman driver reversed into a parking space. I beeped my horn at which McLoughlin, assuming the woman had taken a space I was looking to take myself, began to vehemently hurl abuse at her. Mark looked at him.

"What's your problem, Paul? That's the inspector's wife."

Realising his mistake, he cringed in embarrassment and was close to tears.

On 20 February an urgent phone call came through to my office summoning me to the control room. There I spoke to Dave Gregson and Dave Mitchell over the radio. They were following a car being driven by Miller in the company of Gerry Brown, who ran the Ford Estate. They wanted to know if they should arrest them or follow and report. I said to bring them in straight away. Within twenty minutes both Miller and Brown were in the cells and I went with Dave to interview Miller.

We had never met before, but the arrogance for which he was renowned was absent. I was confronted by a worried man with a young family who knew he faced a long prison term. Before long the gradual pressure applied on him was too much and he came clean, telling us everything.

He had been recruited by Burley towards the end of 1983. Initially, he acted as his courier supplying to dealers on the Woodchurch, but increasingly he became Burley's first lieutenant, supplying dealers all over the Wirral and collecting thousands of pounds a day on his behalf. He confirmed Allen's story about his holiday in the States when Westcott had been left in charge.

On one occasion Miller had been confonted by Burley after we had seized drugs from one of his dealers. Although there was no doubt where the drugs had gone, Burley insisted thay still had to be paid for. He was later picked up by two of Burley's men and taken to a quiet spot off the M53 near Bidston. He was tied to a tree, beaten and fired at. He was convinced he was to be murdered.

"Fuckin' pissed meself, didn't I." Eventually he was released and told he had to pay Burley £1500 within two weeks.

This was a delicate stage in the enquiry. If we could have Miller testify, his evidence would be devastating to Burley. Now he was in custody, he began to visibly relax. Due to the complexity of the cases, Miller would stand trial before Burley. Therefore, he could extract from us an arrangement in which we would approach the judge in chambers and let him know of his co-operation.

This undoubtedly would lead to a lighter sentence. The problem was that Miller could then say what he liked at Burley's trial. It was a matter of judgement and several members of the squad insisted we should bury Miller and give him nothing.

I decided to follow my instincts and deal with him.

I went with Dave to see Brown, but he was so high on drugs he was impossible to talk to. He had made the fatal mistake of the breadhead and started sampling his own wares. Released on police bail, he came back a few days later with his head clear. He denied everything and seemed quietly confident we had nothing on him. When he was arrested and kept in custody, he was visibly shaken. He had, he said, spoken to a 'friend' of his within the police force who told him that unless we had actually caught him in possession, he could not be charged. He needed to be re-educated. He later pleaded guilty and was sent down for five years.

Brown was not prepared to stand up in court against Burley, but he did provide us with a lot of useful information. He would not talk to us in Risley, so we had to pretend he was required for an identification parade in Birkenhead. The Prison Officers were left outside while he gave us what we needed. When we brought him out we feigned frustration at his apparent refusal to take part in

the parade and told the prison officers to take him
back. It worked so well that one of the officers
told Brown to watch himself.

"They'll have it in for you now, lad!"

Wescott was next and proved not to be of the
calibre of those around him. He told us all about
the Allen incident when Miller was in the States
and that Burley had threatened to blow his legs
off if he found him to be lying. He was terrified
of Burley, but never saw him again after that.

During this time, if I wasn't talking to a prisoner
I was on my way to meet one. The tactic of taking
Burley out first was reaping rich dividends. Many
of those dealers still on the run were carrying
firearms to enforce their position and a battle was
raging as vacant positions were being filled and
others struggled to hold on to what they had.
The supply networks on the Woodchurch, Ford
and Moreton estates had been shattered. Thomas
Francis who had recently emerged running the
Birkenhead section of the network was also in
custody. He, too, admitted supplying.

The whole thing was collapsing in on itself. The
biggest and most ruthlessly organised network of
drug dealing in the north-west at that time was
tumbling down. We heard that some Liverpool
'heavies' had come over to the Woodchurch and
were looking for potential witnesses. My immediate concern was for Sandra Coulton. I
telephoned Geoff Rothwell, the Superintendent in

charge of the Force Training Centre and explained the situation to him. Although it had never been done before, I asked if the girl could be accommodated in the residential block there for a few days. He agreed without hesitation and the girl was quickly removed to safety. Another two witnesses were to follow her. I went onto the Woodchurch with Arthur and a few of the lads and put the word out that we knew exactly what was going on and would be waiting around every corner to put a stop to it. The word filtered through and they disappeared. We knew, however, we had to be on our toes. They could reappear at any time.

At this most hectic and important stage of the operation I had four squad members taken from me and transferred back to their sections. Due to the intense activity in certain areas there were others where our presence was limited. Superintendents there asked for their men back. It was too ridiculous and short-sighted for words, but I had to submit to it. The more rural areas were where many of the more successful dealers lived and where many drug-related crimes were commited. I was, though, getting used to this attitude from senior officers not directly involved in our investigations.

By this time, we knew the trial of Burley and Newman would not take place for several months. They were both released on a bail of thousands of pounds in May. The trial was to be the last chapter in a story that had begun in August. Since then we had in twelve months arrested 1,178 people of whom 208 were dealers. 504 search warrants had been executed and prison sentences totalling more than 300 years had been passed down. The price of heroin on the street had risen from £70 a gramme to £140 a gramme. It was a record of which any police officer could be proud.

We were.

17

The trial of Peter Burley and Richard Newman finally got under way on 10th February 1986, twelve months after their initial arrest. Attending the opening day, I found that two Queen's Counsel were appearing for the defence: Mr Maguire, QC for Burley and Mr Somerset-Jones for Newman. Both were assisted by their junior Counsel, Messrs Isaacson and Georges respectively. Mike Wolff representing the Crown, was alone and faced a formidable team.

I had prepared a file several inches thick containing the statements of forty witnesses. Several were directly involved in the supply of drugs in some way and many could testify to being present when Burley was personally involved in trading. We were able to connect him, and Newman, to the selling of illegal drugs over a sustained period of time.

The trial was intense and bitter from the outset. In the case for the prosecution, every shred of evidence was contested and analysed by the defence. I was to be the last prosecution witness to appear and was unable to watch this part of the trial and not able to discuss it. Whatever the public may think, this is strictly adhered to. It would be a nonsense to lose a vital prosecution witness because of a foolish indiscretion. Defence counsel had been known to ask loaded questions to see if the witness was aware of detail that could only have been revealed at the trial.

Instead of sitting outside the court for endless hours, I made myself available to Mike to fetch and carry whatever papers or documents were required by the court. I made countless visits to stations all over the Wirral retrieving journals and files.

Civilian witnesses were the first to appear, but it was impossible for me to know how they had fared or, in certain cases, if they had kept their word. Late on Wednesday, the first police officers were called to the stand and finally, the following day, I was called myself. I took the oath, a deep breath and braced myself.

My own part went well enough. Mike steered me through the relevant points in my testimony and then I was cross-examined by Maguire and Somerset-Jones. Giving evidence in a major trial is always a traumatic experience and I was never completely at home doing so. I was, though, experienced enough to pick my way past the traps laid by the defence counsel and when it was over I was satisfied I'd done my bit. The first part of the trial was over and I was now able to talk to Mike. He thought it had gone just about as well as it could. Each witness had been searchingly examined by the defence and had to resist a fierce attack on their credibilty. Maria Brooke and Paul Sinnot had, as I had hoped, proved invaluable witnesses and their evidence had been particularly damaging to Burley. They each spent a great deal of time on the stand but were, apparently, articulate and well-balanced in their delivery.

A tactic of the defence was to accuse those serving prison sentences of co-operating with the prosecution to receive lighter sentences. It was here I was rewarded for trusting these people. Mike was clearly able to make the point in each case that they had each now been sentenced and nothing could be done if they decided not to testify.

I was particularly pleased that my trust in Miller had been vindicated. He gave clear, precise and damaging evidence. Wescott confirmed that he had acted on Miller's behalf and received drugs from Burley. The most dramatic moment in that first week however came during the testimony of Sandra Coulton. In a sarcastic rebut to one of her answers, one of the Queen's Counsel looked up to her smiling.

". . . and yet you would have to concede, would you not Miss Coulton, that you yourself are really no more than a smackhead?"

She paused only briefly before replying.

"Yes," she said firmly, before pointing a finger directly and unmistakably at Burley, ". . . and he made me one!" A devastating answer.

The defence then opened and Burley took the stand. He was impeccably dressed in a dark suit and denied the charges, refuting all the evidence given to that point. He gave the impression of being a small business man, selling cars and making ends meet and that for reasons he did not understand he was being persecuted by the police. When questioned by Maguire, QC, I thought he did well, but now it was Mike's turn. He took him through his lifestyle, his gambling and the thousands of pounds that had passed through his bank accounts. He pursued Burley every bit as meticulously as we had done. The longer it went on, the more flustered and belligerent Burley became. At one critical moment the gangster in him broke through and the jury were able to see the menace and hostility of the man as he pointed a threatening finger at Mike. It was a magnificent performance by Mike, best of the many impressive displays he gave.

So good was he that when Newman was due to

stand, there were hurried whispers before Somerset-Jones announced that Newman would employ his right not to give evidence. He had no desire to go through the same interrogation suffered by Burley. It had been advocacy of the highest order.

Late in the trial, the defence introduced a transcript of the conversation that had taken place between Arthur and Burley through the cell door at Birkenhead Police Station on the day of his arrest. They wished us to accept it as it stood, but I refused and asked how long they had spent on it. When they replied 'ten hours', I asked for the same and they reluctantly had to agree. As it was Friday this in effect meant we had the tape for the weekend. I left the court with Arthur and went to Dixons, a branch of which was in Lord Street, a few hundred yards away. Knowing that my own home system was not up to scratch, I produced my warrant card and explained to the store manager what I needed. He was happy to oblige and I took home with me a 'top of the range' stereo system from which I was able to produce a transcription revealing more than the defence counsel had intended. The hi-fi system, I hasten to add, was returned on the Monday.

At the end of the second week, both sides summed-up at length and the judge advised the jury on matters of law. The trial was over and the twelve members of the jury retired to consider their verdict.

I had learned over the years it was impossible to correctly forecast which way a verdict would go. I had lost cases I thought were in the bag and won others when I thought 'not guilty' was a formality. In many ways, this had been an even contest.

The jury was out for most of the day and just as it looked like going into another day, we heard that a verdict had been reached and the jury were coming back in. They were very tense moments and I can put my hand on my heart and say I had no idea which way it was going to go. Arthur's 'bottle' had deserted him and he had gone back to Manor Road, extracting from me a promise that I would ring as soon as I had the verdict.

The Clerk of the Court asked the jury foreman if they had reached a verdict and if it was the verdict of them all. He responded that they had and it was.

"In the case of the Crown versus Peter Burley, on the charge of conspiracy to supply heroin, how do you find the defendent? Guilty or not guilty?"

"Guilty." The relief was enormous. For nearly eighteen months I had chased this man, interrogated him and built up a case against him. Now, the network he had been so merciless and cunning in constructing had collapsed around him. A similar verdict was also returned against

Newman. The allegation of attempted bribery was dismissed.

Prior to sentence being passed I was asked by Somerset-Jones, QC to testify that Newman was in the employ of Burley and not an organising dealer himself. I had some respect for the way he had handled himself over the past year and what I was being asked to say was in fact the truth. I saw no justification in kicking a man when he was down. Later, there were some who didn't agree with me, but I am satisfied I did the right thing.

The jury then heard for the first time of their previous convictions before the two men stood to be sentenced. The Trial Judge, Miss Ann Ebsworth, addressed the pair.

"Those dealing in this profitable criminal trade must expect condign punishment. I am satisfied that Burley was dealing on a very extensive scale, organising bulk supplies to go to wholesale dealers on the Wirral who would in turn distribute it to street level. The fact that you could identify the man at the very top shows how close you were to that level. You maintained your position by a mixture of violence, threat and blackmail. You have shown no remorse and offered no excuse. You are a criminal who has turned to drugs as a profitable trade with a lower risk than in other areas of crime. I sentence you to twelve years imprisonment and order that your car, being used in the transport of illegal drugs, be confiscated." Turning to Newman, she referred to the mitigation given on his behalf and by declining to testify he had not submitted evidence that would have been rejected. She then gave him eight years.

They were the longest sentences handed out for the supply of drugs on the Wirral. Some indication of the confidence his family were maintaining of acquittal was the function room they had hired and the party that had been planned for later that night. Burley would not be there.

I rang the station, but Arthur refused to talk to me until I had given the verdict to Molly Hooper. He was cock-a-hoop. When I got back, he came racing down the main corridor to greet me, picked me up and gave me a kiss on the cheek.

We had started life in the August of 1984 as a rag, tag and bobtail unit pitched in against organised, professional criminals. I am as proud of this investigation as any other I was involved in during my thirty-three years in the force. The commitment, courage and tireless endeavours of those involved is a credit to them as police officers.

I have nothing but the highest regard for them all.

18

After a short illness my father, Tom, fell into a coma and during the early evening of 2nd May he passed away. I had taken compassionate leave from duty and been with him for most of the day, returning home briefly for something to eat. I had just stepped out of the shower when a family member rang to tell me he had died. I contacted my only sister, Imelda, and together we travelled to the family home. He had been a role model to me and, with my mother, had encouraged me to join the police force. A devout Catholic, he had lived for his family and made many sacrifices. My parents had always been there for us and I knew I would miss him terribly.

News of my father's death had filtered out and Arthur was contacted by a reliable source who told him that a dealer we had in custody was trying to put a contract out. His intention was to find out where my father was buried and pay to have the grave desecrated. On his next appearance on remand we went to see him in the presence of his solicitor. Naturally, he denied all knowledge of the plot, but knew we would come looking for him if such a despicable act ever took place. This probably ensured my father had the safest resting place in the cemetery.

Much of the time between Burley's arrest and conviction were spent in preparation for the trial. Dave Ackerley had been transferred to the CID and Paddy and Julie promoted to uniform sergeants, leaving Arthur as the only remaining squad member with extensive knowledge of the major enquiry. He was happy to extend his attachment during this critical period. Dave was replaced by Peter Jones, a solid rugby player, and it was his team, including Arthur, who concentrated their efforts on collecting the statements being stacked up against Burley and Newman.

For the rest of the Squad, as we waited for Burley's trial it was business as usual, although the nature of the game had changed dramatically with Miller's removal. His absence meant that drug supply on the Wirral was now fragmented and disorganised. Dealers were operating in independent pockets and had to be sought out one by one.

The arrests of Burley, Newman and Miller had been widely publicised and our reputation was firmly established. Naturally, we had come to the attention of the chief officer, Ken Oxford. He'd spoken to Richard and instructed him to have me write up a report on the methods and mechanics of the squad. It was, he said, his intention to set up similar squads throughout the force. I was happy with the recognition, but told Richard it would take some time to put together. He let me have two weeks. I saw him a couple of days later and he asked me how it was coming along. "I haven't written a word yet, sir," I told him. "Oh, that's a pity," he answered with a smile, "I've promised the Chief it will be ready for Monday." I resigned myself to another lost weekend.

I was only able to take a few days off work after my father died and on my return I received word that a man was checking me out on the Woodchurch, asking a number of people whether or not I could be trusted. This went on for several weeks without any indication of his intent being revealed.

Eventually, he met a police officer at a religious meeting. Both were born-again Christians. He explained that in the past he had been heavily involved in drugs, but now wanted to do what he could to put right his wrongs. In order to maintain the safety of his family, he needed to talk to someone he could trust. The officer advised him to call me, which he did a short while later. I arranged for him to call into my office in Wallasey the following day.

His name was Gary McNeil and in the company of DCs Martin Colton and Steve Williams, I sat and listened to what he had to tell me. The first thing he did was to hand over an imitation firearm wrapped in a plastic bag. He told us he had for some time been involved in the supply of drugs on a serious scale, but having found God he wanted to confess all and accept any punishment due to him.

I was more than a little sceptical about all this at first, as dealers simply didn't just walk in off the street with their arms raised. Yet his information was dynamite. For two hours he told us of his involvement and first-hand knowledge of dealers handling more than thirty-two kilos of cocaine worth £2,000,000 and similar amounts of heroin, amphetamines and cannabis. The organisation, based in Liverpool, had unlimited resources both here and overseas.

As a former regular soldier and mercenary, he was familiar with firearms and frequently carried a gun to protect himself. He gave details of the source of these arms. A property in Gayton, a green-belt suburb of the Wirral, conservatively estimated to be worth £300,000, was said by him to be owned by a major drug dealer. On a personal visit to this house, he declined the invitation of a night out as he had little money on him.

He was told to go upstairs and help himself from a chest of drawers in one of the bedrooms and there found an incalculable amount of cash. Other drawers were similarly crammed. He helped himself to a couple of thousand pounds and was never asked what he had taken.

By the time he had finished, his statement ran to dozens of pages and the lifestyles he was describing were incredible, even by the standards we were used to. For his part, he had disposed of £350,000 worth of drugs over a comparatively short period. On checking through the names listed, we knew many of them were of interest to the Regional Crime Squad in Liverpool. We were able to verify much of the information he had given us and, as he was prepared to testify, I travelled over to Liverpool and gave them all we had. They confirmed they had an informer who could corroborate much of what McNeil had said. Whether it was due to a lack of manpower, budgetary restraints or insufficient evidence, I was disappointed that nothing ever came of that enquiry in Liverpool. As for McNeil, I heard he had 'lost' God while he was on remand but he couldn't, unfortunately, lose his confession or the evidence he had already given. He was sent down for six years.

Shortly after returning from holiday in the middle of June, Peter Jones told me that his team of Phil Leach, Joan Lomax and Ben had traced

Terry Merson to Wallasey Village. Finding him was a good piece of detective work as he had proven to be a very elusive character. Peter intended to take the house out the following morning.

I looked at the mountain of paperwork on my desk demanding my urgent attention, but I didn't take long to decide that I had no intention of missing out on Merson's arrest. I jumped on board. I first came across Merson a couple of years earlier after he had escaped from prison. I traced his girlfriend and she told me he had already been to her flat but she was expecting him to telephone. He called while I was there and he asked to speak to me when she told him I was there. He wished to give himself up and the following day we met as arranged and I arrested him. The next time I heard of him was when McLoughlin turned out to be wired up and said Merson, with Miller, were behind it. I knew him to have bits and pieces of form, but nothing remarkable.

Peter believed he was now armed and had decided to call in the firearms unit before going over to Wallasey to pick him up. I'd carried a gun on occasions in the past, but wasn't on the same planet as the officers of the firearms unit. They were a formidable unit.

The terraced house where Merson was believed to be staying was in a quiet street off Leasowe

Picture 1: Author Mike Mulloy & his wife Carol on their 25th Wedding Anniversary. Photo by Les Lomax

Picture 2: Chief Constable's Commendation awards following Operation Steeple. Back Row(l to r) PC Ben O'Brien, PC Mo Jones, PC Joe Danher, PC Dave Connor, PC Frank Liston, Front Row: PC Mark 'Hedgy' Gerrard, DI Mike Mulloy, Chief Constable Jim Sharples, Sgt Bob Jones, DC Ron Hankey

Picture 3: Lucerne Gardens and Lynmouth Gardens on the Woodchurc[h] Estate, Birkenhead. The blocks have been much improved in recent years, the Wirral Crime Squad were regular visitors there in the eighties.

Picture 4: Steel bar reinforcements found following a drugs bust at a flat in the notorious Lucerne Gardens on the Woodchurch Estate, Birkenhead.

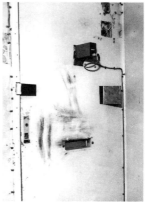

Picture 5: A video system set up b[y] drug dealers to monitor visitors at [a] flat in Lynmouth Gardens on the Woodchurch Estate.

Picture 6: Steel-grill gate discovered following a drugs bust at a flat in Cleveland Gardens, Birkenhead.

Picture 7: The Junction of Bedford Road and Highfield Rd, by Rock Ferr Station. Drug trading was monitored here as part of Operations Bedford I &

Picture 8: Members of the Wirral Crime Squad after PC Mike McDonough
(uniform) had shaved his beard for charity.

Picture 9: "Smack Hill" - Location of Operation Steeple in the north end of
Birkenhead.

Picture 10: Diane Sindall - her murder in August 1986 brought all investigations of drug dealing on the Wirral to a standstill.

Picture 11: Mike Mulloy under strain during the Diane Sindall murder enquiry.

Picture 12: PC Arthur Cowley.

Picture 13: Chief Constable's Commendation Awards following Operatio
Dial-a-Smack. Front Row (l to r): Author Mike Mulloy, Chief Constable Ji
Sharples, DS Martin Colton. Rear: PC Mike McDonough.

Picture 14: Chief Constable's Commendation Awards following Merse
arrest for drug-dealing and grievous bodily harm. Front Row (l to r): Aut
Mike Mulloy, Chief Constable Jim Sharples, DS Peter Jones.
Back Row: DC Peter Blythe, DS Tony Jopson

Road near Wallasey Village and his car, a brand new Fiesta XR2, was parked outside when we arrived. We waited at the end of the street, the armed unit approached the house, one officer making his way around the back. As he did so he was met by the milkman who dropped a full pint of milk when he saw his gun. He didn't need to be told twice to make himself scarce.

A few doors away a middle-aged man was leaving home for work and, showing some consideration for his still sleeping wife, was using his key to turn the lock as he closed the door. Glancing over his shoulder, he saw three armed officers in full combat gear stalking down the street. He scrambled the key back into the lock and fell into the house, slamming the door loud enough to waken the dead.

Once the officers were in place, they took the house straight away and within seconds the call came that the house was secure and that Merson and his girlfriend were present. We followed them in and Peter told Merson he was being arrested for conspiracy to sell heroin.

The house was searched in the presence of Merson and his girlfriend. He was obviously not living permanently at the house, but refused to give his home address. He was arrested and taken to Wallasey Police Station, along with his car.

Back at the 'nick', Frank Anderson and Paul Heslop set about the task of conducting a thorough search of the car. The glove compartment was examined and found to contain a piece of tissue paper wrapped around a plastic bag containing brown powder. This was subsequently proven by forensics to be heroin. The package was taken to Peter, who was still booking Merson at the charge desk. He showed him the two ounce packet and told him where it had been found. Merson reacted immediately.

"It's been planted! Was I there when you searched the car? No! It's nothing to do with me!" Two dealers recently arrested had turned against Merson and one had revealed that he was seeking to expand his business. Over the past couple of weeks, Peter had heard from several sources that Merson was looking to take over Miller's territory and was prepared to go to any extremes of violence to secure it. To take him out so quickly was good police work on the part of Peter and his team.

Merson's girlfriend, Helen Chadwick, gave us the keys of his flat in Albert Road, New Brighton and from there we recovered an assortment of drugs and weapons.

He was later interviewed by Peter in the company of Colin Matthews, and Peter asked him if he owned the Fiesta.

"Yes and no. It's half my car."

"It's half your car? Which half is yours, the front or the back?" He eventually admitted buying the car, but denied ever having seen the heroin we had recovered. Peter carried on.

"You are living at, or have the use of flat 56, Albert Road, do you not?" Merson said he did not.

"All your clothes, your birth certificate, letters and other documents relating to you are in the flat."

"I haven't got a flat. I've never even heard of that flat. I don't understand what you're talking about."

"You're making a fool of yourself, son. Surely you know we're not bloody joking, don't you? We've been there and we've brought all your stuff back." He was shown a number of personal items seized during the raid. "Do you want to change your mind?" Merson hesitated before he answered.

"Yes, I've used the flat." Peter pressed on and showed him the bag of heroin and the mirror found to have traces of heroin and Merson's fingerprints. Peter asked him to comment and wasn't surprised when he denied ever having seen it before, even though the house was pro- tected by two Yale locks, the keys to which had been found in his possession. He was asked when he had last used the flat before the day of his arrest.

"Sometime last week."

"There you go, you're lying again. You were

there yesterday at ten to nine in the morning because we watched you."

"Possibly, I don't know." Peter then turned to the purchase of the car, the total transaction being £6,700 in cash.

"Where did you get that?"

"I won it in the casino."

"What sort of amounts have you won?"

"It varies, like. Sometimes I lose a lot, sometimes I win."

Peter then moved on to the weapons.

"What are all the knives and coshes for?"

"I collect things like that."

"And that?" Peter showed him a large knife in a scabbard.

"That was found by the side of your bed."

"A lot of people make threats towards me."

"A lot of people make threats towards you? I've heard it's the other way round myself. You make a lot of threats towards other people." The interview was coming to a close, but first it was put to him that he had used the flat to cut heroin and that the equipment found was used in connection with dealing. When the items were read to him, he shook his head.

"Everything that a junkie uses."

"Everything that a dealer uses."

"I thought dealers used scales and things like that." No scales had been found.

"That's the only thing you've got us on, Terry."

"I haven't got you on anything."

"Scales, that's the only thing that's missing. You're right."

The interview was terminated and he was later charged, remaining in custody.

Some days later the owner of the property in which Merson had been staying called in to check it out. On entering the bathroom, he noticed that the carpet had been disturbed and on lifting it up, noticed that two floorboards had been cut through. Underneath he found a metal strong box which he handed over to us. When we opened it we found all the usual drug paraphernalia and . . . a set of scales. If Peter was less than pleased with the officer responsible for that part of the search, he was delighted with the scales. It was the missing link and we had been lucky.

Even more damning was the presence in the box of an address book containing Burley's home telephone number and other documents that any reasonable person would see could only relate to drugs and their prices. As a *coup de grace*, one of the keys on Merson's keyring had opened the box. Peter was a happy man.

A few weeks later, he appeared at the Birkenhead courts and had some clean clothing brought in. The clothes he had been wearing were passed in a bag to his solicitor but were first checked by an astute Bridewell officer, John Hulley. Inside the jacket was a letter which Merson made a grab for.

He tried to swallow it, but after a fierce struggle lasting a full minute, John was able to restrain Merson and recover it.

The letter was addressed to 'Peter' and contained several veiled threats. After briefly outlining the charges against him, it stated that if the case against him was proven, he stood to go down for five years. It went on that he had been offered a deal and that 'Peter' was the name at the top of the list. He stated that he would not do a deal but that the intended recipient should not 'fuck about'. He would say that he and 'Peter' had never met if he received £1,000. The letter finished asking for the 'poxy grand' to be paid to 'the kid who delivers this' and was signed 'Franky's mate'. We had no idea who Franky was, but it didn't take a great detective to work out that Peter was Burley.

When later asked about the letter, Merson denied it was meant for Burley, saying he was doing someone else a favour. He was further remanded in custody and for the time being I forgot all about him.

19

Sergeant Alan Jones arrived on the squad and during the mid-summer weeks of 1985 was concentrating his team of Al Green, Peter Allerston and John Smith's efforts on the Bedford Road area of Rock Ferry, a mile to the south of Birkenhead town centre. For a couple of months we'd noticed that there was little drug trade now taking place indoors; our success had literally forced dealers onto the street. Dealing on street-corners with strategically placed look-outs made it more difficult to carry out a raid and presented better opportunities for escape. In addition, heroin was carried in plastic bags which could be swallowed quickly if our presence was noted.

Most of the trade in this particular operation was taking place at the junction of Bedford Road and Highfield Road opposite the Rock Ferry Mersey rail station. The location offered easy access to addicts and the lads, situated in one of the few flats that overlooked the area, had been watching the business develop for a couple of weeks.

The operation had initially been given the code name Wirral, but since our activities were now broken up into separate, independent enquiries, I decided to give each investigation its own identifiable title. The name Wirral was obviously impractical, so the job became Operation Bedford.

Photographs were taken and helped to establish the personalities involved. Informants and other contacts identified faces and Alan's team soon established the organiser to be James Wren, a former associate of Burley and Merson. Friday afternoon appeared to be the busiest period involving several dealers at the same time. The following week Alan decided to move. For most of his team, it was their first big operation, so I was down there with them. It poured down all morning and, while the team were dotted around the area, I was stuck in the car with Arthur.

Eventually, we started to pick up addicts after they made their purchases and were out of sight of the dealers. Several arrests were made and then Alan gave the word to move in on the dealers. In an operation of this kind, speed is of the essence. We had to take them before they realised what was happening. The rain in fact helped us as they were paying little attention to what was going on around them.

An unmarked car containing three officers drove to where one of the dealers was operating. Two officers left the car and hustled the dealer back into it before anyone was aware what was going on. This manoeuvre was repeated until finally we had a total of thirteen people in custody. They were taken down to Birkenhead Police Station. That was the good news. The bad news was that barely any heroin or cash was found. The team were understandably disappointed and not a little confused. It transpired that the courier was stuck in Liverpool kicking his heals waiting for a delivery.

The interviews were now of paramount importance. Two of the arrested men were twins, Robert and David Kinealy, and Robert interested me. He was bright and articulate and seemed condescending in his attitude to the officers dealing with him.

When I brought this up with Alan I was told he had won a place at Exeter University and was due to start there in September. Alan was convinced both he and his brother were dealers.

I sat in with Alan when Robert Kinealy, with his solicitor, was interviewed and while Alan went through the preliminaries I examined the rolls of photographs that had been taken over the last couple of weeks. Kinealy's face was present on many of them, and he looked over at me.

"What's that you're looking at?"

"I'm looking at photographs of you." He appeared stunned and folded almost immediately.

He told us the system for delivery and collection, the names of the couriers and that it was run by Wren. His brother was a housebreaker and, ironically, he talked him into dealing to keep him out of trouble. He was honest enough to admit his motive was greed. Armed with this information, gaining confessions from the others was a formality. When we were done, four were charged with dealing and the rest on lesser charges.

Later that morning Wren was picked up. He denied all accusations vehemently, but before he was charged he asked to see me. He was in a bad way, sweating, shaking and looking ill. He asked if we could do a deal so he could get bail but I refused point blank. With Ben O'Brien I cautioned him but he kept on talking, even after I reminded him it could be used in evidence. In return for bail, he offered us the names of suppliers of drugs and firearms in Liverpool. He had a heavy habit for two years and was desperate to be 'fixed', but we had good reason not to let him out. He would have been dealing immediately he saw the light of day.

At the subsequent trial, everybody except Wren pleaded gulity.

He denied the conversations with myself and Ben had ever taken place. We were solid when cross-examined and on balance I think the jury were going our way. I was confident he would be convicted. Unfortunately, one officer made a bad mistake in giving his evidence and the case was thrown out. Wren was a very lucky man that day, but I consoled myself, and the offending officer, with the fact that he was a serious addict and would be back. Kinealy, his brother and the other two dealers all got three years.

Prior to sentencing the four dealers, His Honour Judge Whickham called me back onto the stand and I gave evidence that all those in the dock had been given the opportunity to make full statements but that they had declined. On passing sentence, he suggested that had they been prepared to co-operate their sentences might well have been lighter. This was covered by the local press with the dramatic headline:

"SHOP THE PUSHERS!"

It gave a clear message that those who helped us would receive leniency from the courts, but that those who refused could expect no sympathy.

With this first post-Burley operation behind us we continued to mop up and bring in dealers operating independently. In some ways the work was more difficult and taxing because there was so little interrelation between different sources of supply. A year earlier, arresting men like Wren and Kinealy would lead us onto other dealers. Now, as each small ring was cleared up, we had to start again. The change in trading methods also meant we had to resort to time-consuming periods of surveillance and arrests became more difficult. Still, we were adapting well and the newer members of the Squad were quick to learn.

Just as a degree of normality was settling in, we were again dealt a bombshell from within the force. The squad was to be reduced to a 'strength' of eighteen men, a loss of ten officers. I was dismayed beyond words. It seemed to be generally believed that, now the network had been smashed, we could operate efficiently with a much smaller squad. In fact, the volcano was simmering and waiting to erupt again. If we could have driven home our advantage at that time for a sustained period, I'm sure we could have brought about a permanent reduction in the abuse of drugs.

It was beginning to dawn on the criminal element that drug dealing on the Wirral meant prison. Looking at the way drug abuse is spiralling out of control today, a decade later, I would argue that a genuine opportunity to overcome drug dealing as a major problem in society was missed in the summer of 1985. Obviously, it will never be eradicated completely, but I doubt if the police will ever again be presented with a similar chance. The success of the methods used on the Wirral may well have been employed elsewhere. As it was, I had eighteen men and I got on with the job as best I could.

20

On Friday, 30th August 1985, Merson escaped from custody. He had appeared at Wallasey for committal proceedings and extra security had been placed around him as he had already made a successful escape bid once before. He was committed after oral proceedings and was returned to the court's cell complex from where he was to be transferred to Birkenhead before being removed to Risley. He was taken to Birkenhead by Arthur, Mike Craven and Ronnie Cashin.

The acting-sergeant there told them to return to the cells underneath the court to await transport to Risley with the other prisoners. Arthur informed him that he had been instructed by his inspector, namely me, that as a security risk Merson was to be lodged at Birkenhead and that was where he was staying. They left him there and came back to Wallasey, but the sergeant, who obviously knew better, walked him back over to the court cells.

When the van arrived, Merson was handcuffed to another prisoner, Alec McDermott, and led out of the building into the enclosed yard. In the yard was a ladder propped against the wall left behind by workmen. Merson needed no second bidding and the handcuffed pair were up and over it in seconds and hot-footing their way down Hamilton Street.

We were told shortly after it happened and I got onto the senior CID officer on duty straight away to ask him for some assistance in mounting an immediate search of the area and their known haunts. He 'generously' offered me the use of his men for an extra half-hour, the stupidity of which took my breath away. As the search developed over the next few days, he was made to pay out a great deal more in overtime.

When Arthur heard of the escape and the circumstances that led to it, he went through the roof.

"That acting-sergeant had better join Equity! He's gonna be acting for the rest of his fuckin' life!"

Arthur knew McDermott's mother was a born-again Christian and compelled to tell the truth. I mentioned to Arthur that we seemed to be coming across more and more born-again Christians these days.

"Yeah," he answered smiling, "that's why I've always got a packed suitcase and £500 in cash ready at me house."

"What are you talking about?"

"If I ever hear you've found God I'm leaving the country on the first plane out!"

Mrs McDermott didn't know where her son was, but told us the name of the person who had come to the house to pick up some clean clothes for him. She didn't know where he lived either, but pointed to where his brother lived close by. He gave us an address in Moreton, but we feared if we left him he would ring his brother ahead of our arrival. Instead, we took him with us and a short while later arrested his brother. Their mother later complained her son had been kidnapped.

The Moreton brother was interviewed in custody and the following morning just after seven we forced our way into a house in Whetstone Lane, Birkenhead and found McDermott under a mattress in a spare bedroom. He struggled briefly but was soon arrested. There was no sign of Merson.

When McDermott appeared in court much later, we had heard whispers that he had made a complaint of being assaulted when he was arrested. I went to the court with Arthur and Paul Fearon and on entering the lift met with a superintendent from Complaints and Discipline with his sergeant, usually referred to as the 'Bag Man' because he carried all the cases. I wished them both good morning and asked them which case they were attending.

"I can't tell you," he said pompously. On the first floor the barrister for the defence counsel, David Aubrey, got into the lift and we talked together until on the fourth floor we all got out and made our way to the same courtroom. While the C & D officers waited outside in the public area the barrister told us that McDermott had decided to plead guilty and had dropped his complaint. The case was a formality and within minutes he was sentenced and sent to prison. As we left, the superintendent hurried after us realising the case was over.

"What was the result?" he shouted after us. I stopped and turned and looked him in the eye.

"I'm sorry, sir, I can't tell you."

After a couple of weeks, Peter Jones received a postcard from Merson posted at Ringway Airport in Manchester. On the front where three pigs and on the back was a message for Peter.

Jaffa

You're no Sherlock Holmes! You know you planted that ounce, oh sorry, two ounces of scag in my glove compartment. I'd give myself up today but your Guv Mulloy has said he's gonna shoot me! Also claimed that I put those two in the dock. Just as if, you prick!

Merson had no respect for the police, or the truth for that matter, but he was a bigger fool than I thought if he expected a card post-marked from the airport would have us believe he'd gone abroad. He'd have to be a bit cuter than that. The contents were just mischief, and the 'two in the dock' he referred to were two men found dead after their car had been driven into a dry dock near Monk's Ferry. Rumour had it that the deaths were connected with drugs, but all police enquiries had established as nothing more sinister than a tragic accident. I'd had no reason to connect them with Merson.

It was about this time that Burley and Newman were granted bail by a judge in Chambers, but we were convinced that Merson would not be found within five miles of the pair. We continued to look for him and, despite the reduction in our numbers, we were still arresting dealers, if not as many.

Peter Thomas, Phil Leach and Ian Latimer had carried out a bust in Lingham Lane, Moreton and had found drugs strapped to the arm of the suspect. He admitted to working for Merson since April, about six weeks after Burley had been arrested and an indication of Merson's bid to fill the void. I was called in to speak to him when he requested the presence of a senior officer. He told me he regularly supplied heroin to one of the civilian staff employed in the station. He pointed him out, but we didn't pick him up until the informant had gone to Risley. Sergeant Joe Large and I dealt with the offender, who had access to our files, and he was arrested and fined. He was, however, allowed to get his life together and put it behind him.

21

Kenyon Terrace was an old Victorian block of houses situated in Devonshire Road, close to Birkenhead Park. The up-keep of such fine old buildings had long been prohibitive and like many similar properties they had been converted into flats. One of the residents had for some time been suspicious of the activities going on in the front ground-floor flat of the house in which she lived. She contacted Tony Jopson, a new arrival on the squad, and came into to see us. We were joined by Peter Blythe and she told us of callers and disturbances at all hours of the day and night. The pattern she described and her suspicions seemed justified when she gave the names of the couple occupying the flat, Ron and Paula Carey.

I first came across the Careys at a bust in Rock Ferry. They arrived to buy heroin after we had secured the flat and what made this job particularly noteworthy was the array of excuses given by the callers. One had called to buy a motor-bike where no motor-bike existed, another had turned up for a Tupperware party and one lad declared he knew it was a bust but had 'come for a nose'! Many hours later he left the police station a sadder but wiser young man. Ron Carey arrived laden with stolen cheque books and credit cards. He was dressed for a day at the races in a smart suit and carrying a binocular case. It turned out he carried the cards in the case and posed as a German tourist as he went about his illicit business.

Tony set his team to watching the flat and the investigation was given the name Operation Devonshire. Before long it was obvious the flat was being used for supply and a few discreet enquiries revealed that Ron and Paula were dealing on behalf of a man called Timothy Hunter. As was the general trend, he had stepped up his operation with the incarceration of Miller and was supplying the Careys with free heroin in return for their dealing on his behalf.

Hunter was a 'breadhead' and was treating our success as an opportunity to move in, make his name and make his money. We were familiar with his style of arrogance.

Perhaps because we had of late been concentrating our efforts on the street and had only carried out a few house raids, some dealers felt it was now safe to operate again from the comfort of their own homes. Additionally, regardless of our tactics, we were never again going to be able to carry out the quantity of raids we once had due to our diminished numbers. The days of four busts being carried out at the same time seemed heady indeed by this time.

Even so, the method of dealing used by the Careys was blasé to say the least. The prospective customer tapped on the window of the flat and was checked out from behind the curtains, always closed. If the client was recognised he was given a thumbs up and indicated through the main door. He was then allowed into the flat.

Having witnessed flats developing into small fortresses, Arthur and myself found this security system almost comical.

"This'll be a tough nut to crack, Boss!" Arthur suggested, smiling.

"I think you're right, Arth, we'll have to be a bit clever with this one." We obtained a key to the front door from the neighbour who had made the initial report, waited hidden in the corridor until someone was let in and then calmly walked to the flat and announced ourselves.

"Hello, Ron, Paula, how's tricks?"

"Oh, shit!" said Ron.

"You bastards!" said Paula

The flat was searched and drugs, stolen property, cheque books and credit cards were

recovered. An indication of the twilight zone
occupied by addicts and dealers was given when
Ron told us that Hunter might call at any time of
the day or night, and frequently called by at four
in the morning. I was reminded again of the last
bust involving the pair of them when I found a
poem penned by Ron just after it happened.

As we were going home one night,
Our eyes beheld a ghastly sight,
Coming away from our front door,
We saw the Drug Squad, five or more,
We stepped back quick from this intended haul,
But up popped two from behind a wall,
'No Bones Jonesy' and 'Fagsy' Farrell,
"We've got you now, trapped in a barrel,"
Up ran the Squad, simply having a ball,
Exhibit case, handcuffs, sledgehammer and all.
"Don't try to run!" said Leddington Lil,
"We've come to arrest you, we're from the Old
  Bill,
'No Joy' Mulloy is our boss's name,
And this is Barnsey of sledgehammer fame!"
So I pulled out me gear and handed it in,
But they still searched me pad, we just couldn't
  win,
They crashed all over our neat little home,
Every cupboard and drawer and box they did
  comb,
"Stand over here!" "Now sit over there!"

"Pull up the carpet!" "Tip up the chair!"
"Now take your clothes off and show us your
  cheeks,
You gave us your gear, but we still like to peek!
Now, Leddington Lil will frisk down your wife,
And we'll read your mail and nose into your
  life,"
The smiles soon faded when no drugs were
  found,
Nor were there tellies or money around
"For being so straight we'll find you a cell,
And just for good measure, throw your wife in
  as well
You've been very good and you're going to
  confess,
So to show no hard feelings, we'll leave you a
  mess.
So off to the lock-up in convoy we go,"
With the Squad, exhibits and sledgehammer in
  tow,
They bang us up behind a locked door,
But half-an-hour later they come back for more,
"We'll take your prints and have a small chat,
You can tell us about this and tell us about that,
You can give us the names of all your suppliers,
And tell us the truth, we don't like liars,
We know you take smack, smoke pot and fix
  dyke,
But what really bugs us is . . . what is it like?"

Frequently, dealers who were locked up would offer all kinds of information in return for being released on bail, in a similar fashion to James Wren, but the answer was always the same: 'Sorry, the boss says no joy'. Hence the nickname, 'No Joy' Mulloy.

Inside the Careys' flat, the callers started to arrive. They were searched and questioned in the communal kitchen close to the front door. They were then escorted to a vacant bedsit in the basement where Peter Blythe looked after them. So many of the callers were already known to us, the bust began to take on the appearance of an old boys' reunion.

"Hello, Mick, long time no see, how are you doing?"

"Not so bad, Arthur, and yourself?"

"Can't complain, Mick. How's the baby?"

"Baby? She starts school in September."

"You're jokin'! Where does the time go?"

"Beats me, Arthur."

They were each carrying the usual small amount of drugs and knew the score. One woman arrived in possession of dozens of credit cards and it transpired that Casey had turned his talents to the task of 'laundering' the cards by removing the signatures.

The scene was a familiar one. Those who were simply addicts knew that we weren't after them and would not be detained too long. I went below to see how Peter was getting on and could hear the chat going on inside the bedsit.

"Who collared you?" one voice said.

" 'Mad Dog' Cowley," said another.

"Did he beat you up?"

"Yeah, not 'alf!" It was all nonsense, but they were all careful to maintain they had told us nothing until it was beaten out of them. They all confirmed that they had each taken a few belts from Arthur. In the end, there were nearly twenty in the room when the latest arrival joined them, unaware of the rules of the game they were playing.

"Did you tell Cowley what you know?"

"Yeah."

"I suppose he beat it out of you?"

"No, I just told him." The response was a unanimous chorus.

"You fuckin' grass!!"

Hunter turned up late in the evening, but he got wind of what was going down as he neared the front-door. He scarpered in the direction of Slatey Road with four of the lads in pursuit. He was caught a few minutes later in Alton Road near St Anselm's Preparatory School, which I had attended as a young boy. At the station Hunter denied everything. The Careys talked freely in interview, but in court they surprisingly pleaded 'Not Guilty' and the trial lasted several days.

During my evidence, the court was adjourned

for lunch and during the break I overheard the defence barrister, David Aubrey, asking to see my original statement. He was given a copy, but asked again for the original. He made no attempt to conceal his request from me and, indeed, made sure I knew what he was doing. If it was an attempt to test my resolve it worked. Outwardly, I remained calm but my mind was in a turmoil wondering what it might be he thought he had found. Back on the stand, I quickly picked up on the direction he was taking me. He passed me my original statement.

"Could you tell the court the date on your original statement?"

"3rd September 1985."

"3rd September? And yet Mr Cowley has given evidence in his statement, which is dated ... let me see ... 27th August, that he has read and agreed that your statement is a true account of what occurred. How could he possibly have done that, Inspector, when your statement did not on that date exist?"

"It did exist on that date."

"Then please explain to the court how this remarkable occurrence might have taken place."

"At any given time, I might have several bundles of files on my desk. I am usually working on more than one statement at the same time."

"The court is not interested in your excessive workload, Inspector, but are you suggesting you may have been confused by this mountain of paperwork before you?"

"Not at all. As I said, I am often working on several statements at the same time. Therefore, some statements I type myself, others are typed for me by members of the clerical staff using my notes. When they are returned to me it may be some time before I am able to read them through. At the end it is signed and dated in my hand. That is the date I checked it and signed it."

This was the truth, but the barrister had thought he had me and he wasn't letting the matter rest just yet. Arthur was recalled to the stand. If I had tried to explain events in a calm and professional manner, Arthur's method was far more effective. The barrister asked him if he had known me to have several files requiring attention at the same time.

"Have you ever been in the Inspector's office?" was the first part of Arthur's answer.

"The pleasure has been denied me," the barrister told the court sarcastically.

"Well, I have and I don't know how he does it. Have you got any idea how many bundles of files he has all over his office?"

"No idea."

"Dozens! But he knows exactly which one is which. How do you think he keeps track of them all?"

"Please enlighten me."

"Because he knows what he's doing. Have you got any . . . ?" At this point the judge intervened.

"This is all very entertaining," he said, becoming quite irritated, "but I would remind you, Constable Cowley, the normal procedure is for you to answer the questions rather than ask them!"

"I'm sorry, Your Honour." Bob Atherton, counsel for the Crown, fought in vain to keep a straight face.

"Please continue, Mr Aubrey."

"Yes, thank you, Your Honour." The barrister turned back towards Arthur. "What precisely then is the procedure your Inspector follows to introduce some order into the world of chaos that is his office?"

"Well, when he wants a statement sorting out, he'll call an officer into his office. 'Get in here, Cowley,' he'll shout. When I go in, he picks a file up, goes straight to his statement, tells me to read it and asks me if I agree with it. 'If you do,' he says, 'make a statement to that effect and get back on the street!'

I'm not sure how well the jury followed Arthur's testimony, but his passion for telling it was convincing enough and Hunter and the Careys were convicted. Ron and Paula got three years each and Hunter was sent down for four-and-a-half. As I boarded the train with Arthur and Ron Cashin at Moorfields Station, we were confronted by Hunter's mother.

"You fuckin' bastards! Do you think four-and-a-half years bothers our Tim? He'll be out in fuckin' three! He was expectin' six! Three? He'll do three standin' on his fuckin head!" I wasn't about to get involved but said quietly to Arthur that if he was going to do his time standing on his head, why was he crying when he was sent down? Ron laughed.

"Probably the thought of not seeing his lovely mum for three years!"

22

Early in November, an attractive young woman called at the front desk of Wallasey Police Station and asked for me by name. Her name was Sarah Tate. She was the girlfriend of Michael Ellis, Merson's closest and most trusted friend. Although involved in the drug scene himself, Ellis had proven to be resolute in his loyalty to his friend. During the hunt for Merson we had called on Ellis several times but he never told us a thing.

Tate had called at the station to tell us that Merson had been to see her the previous evening and was coming back that night. He wanted to leave the country for a while and was demanding Tate give him a copy of her birth certificate so he could apply for a false passport for his girlfriend. She wanted nothing to do with him and had put him off for a day by saying she would have to go to her mother's house to collect it.

Tate was eight months pregnant and wanted Merson to face justice. Ellis, apparently, had no idea what she was doing and would have had a fit if he found out. She told us that she was expecting Merson some time after seven.

"Will Ellis be there?" I asked her.

"Yeah, probably. He mustn't know why you're there. You'll just have to say it's a routine visit."

"Well, he's had plenty of them. Probably due for another one."

"Look, Michael's got some drugs in the flat. Nothing much, just a bit of coke an' that for himself. I can't touch it, I can't get rid of it before you come. He'll know."

"Let's see what happens first, eh?"

That night I had every available member of the squad in the area of the flat in Wellington Road, near to the New Brighton promenade. I even had the luxury of the assistance of Keith Raybould and Graham Gathercole from the Drug Squad. I wasn't comfortable approaching Merson without firearms, but if we were to carry this off as a routine visit we could hardly turn up armed to the teeth. We would have to rely heavily on the element of surprise; Merson would feel safe approaching Ellis' flat.

I went up to the front door of the flat on the first floor with Tony Jopson, Peter Blythe, Ian Beaumont and Arthur. The rest of the squad were strategically placed around the building ready to move at a moment's notice. Ellis himself opened the door.

"Oh, fuckin' hell, fellas! Don't you ever give up? He's not here, I don't know where he is, I haven't seen him. Anything else?"

"We've got a warrant, Mike, let's have a look round." We went through the motions of searching the flat and found the drugs Tate had told us about.

"You're takin' the piss, Mr Mulloy. You're not gonna charge me for that shit, are you?"

"Let's sit down and talk, Mike." I sat down with Tony while Arthur, Peter and Ian kept Tate company in the kitchen. They certainly had the better looking part of the arrangement. It was a strange evening. We interviewed Ellis at great length but it was difficult to concentrate knowing that Merson might turn up any minute. I told Ellis we would be taking him down to the station, which although it didn't please him, is what he would have expected.

"Let's have a cup of tea first," I suggested, "and see if your old mate drops in." We dragged it out until nearly two in the morning before we gave it up. There was a great sense of anti-climax when we left. Ellis went with us, but as ever, he said nothing.

Shortly after New Year, I was aroused from sleep around one o'clock in the morning by the telephone. The Divisional control room told me a call had been received from Tate. She had returned home a little earlier and as she got out of a taxi saw Merson accompanied by another man being admitted to her flat by Ellis. She left the scene immediately and was now in the company of two officers in a police vehicle parked on the promenade. I neither washed nor shaved and within minutes was on the road to Wallasey.

Tate was very nervous, but adamant that it was Merson she had seen. She showed a lot of guts in coming to us so quickly. I was told the area around the flat was now secure and exits were all under observation.

I was under no illusions as to how difficult it could be to arrest Merson and contacted the duty assistant chief constable to request the presence of a firearms team. We had received numerous reports that Merson was permanently armed and had no intention of risking the lives and health of police officers.

Within an hour, the firearms team were with us and with the assistance of Tate we drew up a plan of the flat to prepare our tactics. Within two hours of Tate's phone call, we were ready to move in. Nobody had left the flat, so unless Merson had left in the minutes before the patrol observing the flat had arrived, he was still there.

We parked up in adjoining roads and made our way to the flat on foot. My adrenalin was pumping and I was dry-mouthed. We gained access to the building using Tate's keys and in the company of firearms officers, made our way to the first floor. Amid a great deal of banging and shouting, we quickly broke into the flat, but all was quiet. There was no sign of Merson or his friend, but Ellis was sitting and crouched forward in a chair. He was covered in his own blood and had severe head and facial injuries. The walls, floors and furniture of the living room, hall, kitchen and bathroom were covered in Ellis' blood. He was barely conscious, but he appeared to recognise me and was trying to speak.

While Ellis was rushed to hospital, I arranged for an scene of crime officer to examine the flat and we began to rouse the neighbours. Incredibly, a young woman occupying a flat on the second floor had heard everything, but instead of ringing the police had gone to bed.

She had been woken by the noise of Ellis' flat being smashed up for more than ten minutes. After hearing footsteps descend the stairs, she heard Ellis sobbing and calling for help. She then heard him drag himself back into the flat and closing the door behind him. After a few minutes silence, she had crept down the stairs to look about. As everything was now quiet, she returned to her own flat and went back to bed. I would never condemn any member of the public who does not want to get involved and I can readily understand the woman's fear. Being on the telephone, though, it is beyond me why she could not make even an anonymous call to the emergency services to summon help.

I spent most of the rest of the night talking to Tate. She was enormously distressed by what had happened to Ellis. It was her worst fear becoming reality and what she had sought to prevent by talking to us. Ellis himself was transferred to the Brain Unit at Walton Hospital in Liverpool and by morning his condition had deteriorated. Apart from a multitude of severe bruises and lacerations, he had sustained a fractured skull and his brain had shifted within the cranium. He was very ill and the hospital staff would not commit themselves on his prospects at this time.

In a meeting of senior officers that morning, I gave the details to the CID command and a joint operation to track down Merson was agreed. One CID officer got the sharp end of my tongue when he suggested an immediate response without firearms may have caught Merson. Apart from being incorrect, I placed too high a value on the men who worked under me to take such foolhardy risks. There was no tact in my response.

"I can be a hero when I'm lying in a bed and some other bugger has to do the dirty work!"

A large number of officers were assigned to the hunt for Merson and after they had been briefed I returned home to catch a few hours sleep. I returned later in the afternoon to oversee the operation and spoke again to Tate.

A number of arrests were made in the course of the enquiry which had no relation to the attack on Ellis. It is inevitable that when police converge on an area in numbers, a great many non-related crimes are cleared up.

The object of the enquiry, though, was Merson. It was an essential matter of public safety that he be taken out of circulation as quickly as possible.

23

During the course of our enquiries, Alan Jones had stumbled onto a smuggling operation that had gone wrong at the French customs at the Calais ferry terminal. Two men and two women had been driving their car through customs prior to boarding the Folkestone ferry when a police dog casually relieved itself over one of the wheels. Admiring his handiwork as only dogs do, he began to howl when his nose encountered a smell he had been trained to recognise. A subsequent search revealed £60,000 worth of cannabis.

One man admitted the offence and, unbelievably, the other three were allowed to continue their journey back to England. When it was discovered that the other man was the son of a major dealer on Merseyside, Alan looked into it. We knew this dealer had connections with Merson. Tate had told us of a conversation between Ellis and Merson where they had discussed a drug deal that had gone wrong about the same time. We weren't sure where it would lead us, but we decided to pick the three of them up.

I went to the address of the other woman with Arthur and Les and she turned out to be completely out of her depth. She was from a good family, had been to a good school and had no previous convictions. She was, though, very naive. We found photographs of the happy foursome taken in Morocco and before long she admitted her part in the smuggling operation and implicated the other two. From documentation found in her flat we were able to confront the other two with receipts for travellers' cheques to the tune of £10,000 and a cash receipt for the £4,000 purchase of a car. Not bad for a couple on Social Security Benefit. As the offences concerned the importation of illegal substances, the case was handed over to the Customs and Excise.

There was no link to Merson and no indication that any of the three had seen sight nor sound of him since the attack on Ellis. We had nothing else to do with them, although we were called on to give evidence at their trial. The male had pleaded not guilty. When the defence opened, the woman arrested by Arthur and myself gave her evidence. In the middle of her being cross-examined, the accused man audibly but clearly muttered "ah, fuck it!" from the dock and beckoned his counsel.

After a short adjournment, he changed his plea to guilty and was given three years. I've lost count of the hundreds of trials I've attended over the years but I have never witnessed anything like it before or since.

We were no nearer Merson. One man we knew to be a close associate was proving elusive, but we finally caught up with him in rather bizarre circumstances. He had been followed when driving through the Kingsway Mersey Tunnel by officers on a routine patrol. Although he wasn't known to them, something must have spooked him. On arrival at the toll booth on the Birkenhead side he abandoned the vehicle and fled the scene. The car was eventually brought to Wallasey Station and found to be clean.

A couple of days later a constable came from the front desk to my office to tell me the dealer was on the phone and asking about his car. Somewhat incredulous, I took the call and identifying myself as the duty inspector asked how I could help. He gave a garbled story about lending his car to a friend of a friend and wondered if he could have it back.

"No problem at all," I told him, "just call into the station and ask for me, Inspector Jones, personally, sign a form and you can drive it away today." He thanked me and said he would be with us shortly. When I told Arthur, he just laughed.

"Oh, yeah? You should have told him to bring

a few mates. Maybe we could organise it so all the druggies in Birkenhead pop in to see us and form an orderly queue outside. They could tell us what they've been up to and we could have them all banged up on the same day! If he turns up, I'll buy the drinks."

"Alright, Arthur! I don't think he'll turn up either. I'm just telling you what he said."

Less than twenty minutes later, the phone went again and it was the same constable at the desk telling me that a gentleman had arrived asking to see the duty inspector personally regarding his car.

"Can anybody lend me twenty quid?" asked Arthur. Before long the man had confessed to being concerned in the supply of drugs and was held in custody.

Ellis' condition was still giving cause for concern. He was at death's door and his family had several times been rushed to his bedside as it seemed his time was up. However, he continued to hang on.

Detective Superintendent Roger Corker was the divisional CID commander in charge of the hunt for Merson and he decided in consultation with myself and other senior officers to publish his photograph in the *Liverpool Echo*. Joe Large had received information that he was living in Liverpool and was armed. Late in January we received two independent phone calls that led us to an address in Anfield and with Tony Jopson, Arthur and several other officers I drove over there. One of the team had gone to school with Merson and was sure he could positively identify him however he might be dressed. Observations on the house in question were maintained for two days until finally he was spotted leaving the house. Throughout that day, his movements were monitored and careful consideration had to be given to the way we should take him. We could not afford to take any action that might draw his attention, but there were generally children playing near to his house. Safety was paramount, but we could hardly clear the street before we moved in.

We waited at a nearby station and tensions grew as the hours passed by. It was decided to go in around midnight and attempt to isolate him within the house. The firearms unit were in place and we were about to make our move when suddenly a report came in that the door had opened and he had left. Roger thought it likely he had gone out drinking and that we should stand down and return in the morning. As the squad began to disperse another call came in saying he was back. Having watched the house for more than forty-eight hours we knew he was on his own.

Within minutes we were in position outside the house and seconds later the front door had gone in. The firearms unit went in first and it seemed almost immediately that a shout came down the stairs.

"Don't shoot me! Don't shoot me!" He was arrested in his bed and I got a lot of satisfaction from sitting with him in the living room while the house was searched. I recognised Arthur's voice shouting in triumph upstairs. Under the floorboards near the bed in which Merson had been sleeping, Arthur found a loaded double-barrelled, sawn-off shotgun. They are the most fearsome of weapons and every officer is delighted when one is recovered and taken off the streets.

As well as masks and other weapons, we found paperwork proving his girl was in America and that he had been considering going there, or to Canada, himself. Another few weeks and he would have been out of the country for a long time. It was the early hours of Saturday morning, 25th January, 1986 and Merson was back in custody. We all made damned sure he was going nowhere this time. He was taken to the nick back at Wallasey and I made my way home for a few hours sleep.

The following morning, after a relaxing breakfast which we thought we deserved, Tony Jopson and I conducted a formal taped interview with Merson and his solicitor. Not surprisingly, he denied all the offences put to him, with the exception of having been in illegal possession of a firearm. Later in the day, he was charged and kept in custody on a number of charges.

In addition to supplying heroin, he was eventually to be indicted with aggravated burglary, robbery, grievous bodily harm, actual bodily harm, possession of a sawn-off shotgun and two counts of threats to kill and demanding money with menace. The latter charges were to be left on file, but this was all in the months to come.

24

It was by now late February, 1986 and with the Burley trial behind me I was looking forward to a break with Carol to recharge my batteries. In preparation, I was clearing my desk so I wouldn't have to return to a mountain of paperwork. The end of the leave year was approaching so the station was fairly quiet with an above average number of officers taking their leave entitlement. Two of the lads on duty were Ron Cashin and Alan Wilkes who had gone over to Liverpool following up an enquiry on some indecent photographs found in the developing department of a fast photo processing shop.

Apparently, photographs handed in by customers were now processed by computer and not necessarily seen by the staff, but in order to maintain quality control there are random checks made and were done at the administrative office of the shop which was in Wallasey and, therefore, came under our jurisdiction. A film had been handed in by a member of the public which contained indecent photographs of two young girls. The processing department had informed the police.

The address given with the film turned out to be false. It wasn't something we normally got involved with, but the lads themselves were both parents and keen to pick this pervert up. I let them get on with it. They had been watching the shop for a few days, waiting for the person concerned to pick up the photographs. It had gone on longer than I could really afford and if I let it run much longer they would have exhausted my almost non-existent overtime pool. They, equally, were keen to carry on, so we came to a deal where they would continue the observations in their own time, but if they picked him up and charged him, they could submit the hours and be paid. To this they readily agreed.

I was still hard at my paperwork around mid-morning when Martin Colton came into my office and mentioned that Ron and Alan had locked somebody up in the Bridewell and wanted to talk to me. I finished the report I was working on and then made my way to see them. As I passed the main office, I called in to answer a persistently ringing telephone and saw Martin driving from the station at considerable speed. I assumed he was late for an urgent meeting, replaced the receiver and made my way to the cell area.

When I entered the charge office, both Ron and Alan were looking particularly subdued. At the charge desk was a man in his late thirties, sitting with his head in his hands and clearly crying. I was taken to one side and as the story unfolded I could now see why Martin had been in such a rush to get off the station. He was determined not to get drawn in to what is always an unpleasant business for the police; Ron and Alan had arrested a fellow police officer.

When he was picking up the photographs, the pair had approached him and identified themselves. At this, the man had run out of the shop but didn't get very far before he was caught. He then revealed he was a serving Merseyside Police officer with fifteen years service and begged Ron and Alan to say he had eluded them and to let him go. When I spoke to him, he gave me his rank as constable. I asked where he was posted and where he lived, which he told me. I examined his warrant card which was in a sealed property bag. Like Ron and Alan, I felt very despondent at having to deal with this, but they were, of course, absolutely right to bring him in. I decided Richard Adams should be told straight away.

I had never before been involved in such a case and I admit to being keen to pass it on. Such crimes were usually dealt with by either the internal Complaints and Discipline Department or, more likely on this occasion, the CID. I found Richard in the officer's mess and called him outside. We went to his office and I gave him the details. He asked me to stay while he rang the Chief Superintendent of the C & D Department and I acted as a go-between as I was asked a series of questions by the Chief Superintendent. It soon became obvious to me that the name of the officer concerned was already known to the officer, which surprised me given that the force numbered some 4,000 men. I was then asked to leave by Richard so the the two officers could speak privately.

When I was called back some ten minutes later, Richard told me I was to take charge of the enquiry. I couldn't believe my ears. The C & D had a number of superintendents, many of them detectives, and in any case this was a CID matter. When I put this forward, Richard told me the decision had been made at the highest level and that I was to deal with it immediately. He added that he wanted to be kept informed of my progress as and when anything developed. As a last resort, I explained I was due for several days leave, which I would lose if I didn't take them before the end of March. I had several court appearances to make and taking this enquiry would make it impossible to take my leave before the passing of the requisite time limit. Richard assured me the necessary approval from head-quarters would be forthcoming, allowing me to carry those days over into the next leave year.

I asked Joe Large to assist me and, although less than thrilled with the idea, he knew somebody had to do it. When we first spoke to the arrested officer in the presence of his solicitor he proved very difficult to deal with. He admitted taking the photographs but would not reveal the identity of the two young girls. When asked why, he said he wished to explain his actions to the girls' parents first. This, as he very well knew, was complete nonsense and I was never going to allow it, but still he refused to let us know who they were.

I decided to have his home searched and with Joe, Paul Fearon, Ian Beaumont and several other officers we made our way to his house on the outskirts of Liverpool. We found large quantities of ladies underwear, bundles of obscene maga-zines containing ten-year-old girls and a large quantity of photographs of young girls in various states of undress. We found a spyhole had been drilled above the bathroom and a room had been fitted out as a studio. This was the same room as had appeared in the first batch of photo-graphs we had recovered.

Back at the Wallasey station, I went with Joe to the bar for a quick orange juice and a bite to eat. The whole place was buzzing with the 'scandal', but the bar fell silent as we entered. The conversation slowly picked up again and as we waited to be served we were approached by a detective of many years service. I steeled myself for a verbal confrontation, but I needn't have worried.

"Look, Boss," he said, "you should know we were talking about you, but not against you. This is about kids and the bastard deserves everything he gets. He doesn't deserve to wear the cloth."

We went to see the suspect again later that evening, again in the presence of his solicitor. He had had time to think things through and almost immediately gave us the names and addresses of the two girls in the photographs. They were both fourteen and lived in Speke near to the airport on the south side of the city. He would not agree that the pictures were obscene, although he conceded they were under age. He fell silent when I asked him how he would feel if it was his own fourteen-year-old daughter posing in that way.

I had no female squad member on duty, so I called in Cath Stanley from Birkenhead who joined myself and Joe when we travelled to Speke to visit the homes of the two girls. We were initially confronted with anger, but Cath did a very good job in diffusing a delicate situation and getting the statements we needed. One of the girls was the officer's God-daughter and the other her friend. They told us they often stayed for the weekend and had been puzzled when he insisted they take a bath. They had heard a camera clicking, but had not known they were being photographed. Having slowly persuaded them to undress for the camera, he had threatened to show their parents the pictures if they ever said anything.

Speaking to the mother of the girl who was a friend of the God-daughter, it turned out she did not even know the address of the officer where her daughter stayed.

"Isn't that a bit unusual," I asked her. She very quickly put me in my place.

"For God's sake, he's a police officer!"

We now had enough evidence to charge him and made our way back to Wallasey. Despite it being past midnight, the senior duty officer was waiting for us when we got back to the station. The arrest of a police officer is no small matter and he had been ordered by Richard to await us and see the matter through. I typed out the charges and, although I had no sympathy for him, it was with a heavy heart that I charged a fellow police officer with a criminal offence. He was later bailed for committal proceedings to the Crown Court.

It turned out that he had a history within the force of making complaints against supervising officers, very senior officers and the C & D themselves. It had been for this reason the Chief

Superintendent already knew him and had wanted somebody else to deal with it. I only wish I had been given such a choice.

While he was out on bail he was arrested again in Liverpool. This time, incredibly given the circumstances, for indecent assaults on young girls aged ten to twelve. He finally appeared before Mr Justice Wood and pleaded guilty to all the charges against him. In passing sentence the judge told him "young girls need to be protected from your activities for a very long time" and gave him eight-and-a-half years. I have to confess the length of the sentence surprised me. It was the longest I had known to be passed on a serving police officer, but, of course, his service was irrelevant to the case and the sentence.

True to his word, Richard had supported my application to have my leave carried over to the next leave period. A terse reply came back from Assistant Chief Officer Alison Halford refusing my request on the grounds that I had not made out a proper case. I wondered how many days she had sacrificed through making arrests and attending court from behind her desk.

25

Although we were determined that Merson would be given no opportunity to escape, that did not guarantee that he would not try. In May, he was being transferred from Birkenhead Magistrates Court to Risley Remand Centre in a mini-bus with his escort and another prisoner.

As they travelled along the M62 motorway, Merson suddenly produced from his waistband a sliver of glass fashioned into a knife and held it at the throat of the officer handcuffed to him after head-butting him to the floor.

"Stop this bus or I'll kill the bastard! I mean it! Do as I say or I'll kill him!"

Showing great courage and presence of mind, the senior prison officer ordered the civilian driver to accelerate and a violent struggle ensued. Merson was eventually overcome and disarmed. When he later appeared in court, charges of threatening to kill and assault occasioning actual bodily harm were added to the growing list. We had already linked him with an aggravated burglary that had taken place in Heswall the previous November after forensic evidence at the scene tied in with a pair of shoes found in his possession.

Distractions of one kind or another were part and parcel of running a regional crime squad, and on another occasion I was asked to assist with manpower by Peter Burns, the superintendent at Hoylake, in observing and subsequently raiding a wine bar where the licencing laws and fire regulations regarding capacity were being blatantly abused. I was happy to co-operate with Peter. He was a good friend with a very dry sense of humour.

He was one of the old school and, quite rightly, proud of the fact that he had nearly forty years unbroken service in the force. He once told me of an occasion when he was enduring his annual appraisal in the hands of a comparatively young assistant chief officer who had been promoted from a force down south. He was telling me that he thought experience was not the be all and end all of qualification for high rank.

"Yes, sir, I do agree with you," Peter replied, gritting his teeth, "but if you and I were unfortunate enough to be lying side by side in hospital suffering from the same life-threatening complaint, could I, with all due respect, have the experienced surgeon to operate on me?"

The main job in hand, though, was chasing the dealers and now that Miller's operation had been shut down, most of our work was on the streets. As each pocket emerged, we would close in and close it down. The most experienced team I had at this time was led by Tony Jopson and included Frank Thomas, Al Rushton and Peter Blythe. Peter's favourite trick was to have postcards, bearing nothing but a white spot, sent to me from all over the world. I never found out how he organised it. Tony's team had been watching a house in Ravenscroft Road near Birkenhead's Charing Cross and almost directly opposite the house in which Carl had been born and raised. The address was occupied by a young girl and her boyfriend and a succession of known criminals, mostly burglars, had been seen coming and going.

After the usual observations from the upper-floor of a flat on the other side of the road Peter decided to go in. Through binoculars, the lads had watched the woman cutting heroin with her two young children happily playing alongside her. On occasions, they had seen her leave the room for several minutes leaving the deadly powder, blades and syringes with the children. After the raid, we had the two occupants, four visitors and the usual amount of drugs and cash. We also recovered a large quantity of stolen credit cards, cheque books and family allowance books.

The woman, who I knew, was twenty-seven and had been addicted to heroin for more than five years. She was divorced but her husband, and the father of her two children, had been put away some time earlier for dealing. The children, the real victims of this, were put in the hands of the social services. Her current boyfriend had only recently been released from prison for dealing.

One of the visitors we had arrested came up with an original story. He had, he said, never been an addict and never been involved in dealing. It was only when he watched his brother become addicted that he decided to infiltrate the drug gangs and accumulate the evidence that would put them away. Keith Raybould and Graham Gathercole, who interviewed him, were very impressed.

His father, he went on, was a successful local businessman and they lived in a very respectable part of Bromborough near the police station. When asked, though, to produce the first part of his conscientious plan to rid the area of dealers, he was not prepared to name or locate his sources and admitted he had made considerable financial gain from his activities. After listening to this entertaining twaddle for about half-an-hour, he was returned to his friends in the cells and all were later charged.

A few weeks later, they all successfully, and somewhat surprisingly, applied to the Crown Court for bail. Within a short period of time, Arthur found out they had each immediately returned to dealing. By coincidence, on that evening, we had the same team armed with a warrant close-by who had to pull off a raid. As absolutely no activity had been sighted and we were in possession of a back-up warrant for Ravenscroft Road, Arthur suggested we drop in.

The entire team made straight for the address. We went right through the front door, only hastily repaired since our last visit, as soon as we arrived. We found all we had expected to and the woman, only recently re-united with her children, was on her way back to prison. This time there would be no bail.

She was on a hiding to nothing when she was being sentenced and her barrister asked me if I was prepared to say that she was a loving mother who cared very much for children. Despite her carelessness with the drugs in her home, I knew this to be the case, so before the judge passed sentence I testified that she was torn between her love for her children and her desperate need for heroin. I also added that she felt guilt and shame at her inability to properly care for her children. The judge, I believe, was not even remotely influenced by my soft words, as he gave the girl five years. The 'infiltrator' and the boyfriend received the same.

I thought nothing more about it until I read in a local paper a year later that she had successfully appealed against the length of her sentence. The appeal court ruled that the trial judge should have taken into account what I had said and her sentence was reduced to three years.

Only a few months later she was released on parole and she rang the office and asked me to meet her in a pub in Wallasey. I agreed, but being naturally suspicious I took Di Ethelstone with me. Di had only recently arrived, but she would go on to prove to be one of the most effective officers in the unit.

The woman we met was well-dressed and free of drugs. She was with her children again and trying to re-build her life. She told me she had conducted her own appeal and without being able to quote my words in court, she would have failed and still been in prison. She wanted to meet me just to say thanks.

I would be less than honest if I do not admit that I gleaned some satisfaction from this meeting, but it was short-lived. Within weeks I heard she was back on heroin and her efforts had been for nothing. I'd seen it so many times before, I scolded myself for thinking she could be one who would make it.

There were many lighter moments to give relief.

On one occasion, Arthur placed an unfamiliar bunch of keys on his desk.

"What are they for?" I asked him.

"They belong to Frank Singleton," he answered. Frank was a petty thief and an addict, but was so courteous and inoffensive when he was arrested that we'd all grown quite fond of him. He was in court every five minutes and the moment he was released he was soon on his way back again.

"So why have you got Frank Singleton's keys?"

"We turned him over again this morning. It's the third time we've kicked his door in since Christmas and he said, as we're costing him a fortune in repairs, could we let ourselves in next time."

About this time, Richard was promoted to assistant chief constable. I was sorry to see him go as I was always able to trust and rely on him. He was, though, always destined for higher rank and on his last day he called me into his office. He thanked me for the work I had done and we both laughed when he brought up the fact that my returning to my section in Birkenhead now seemed a distant and long-forgotten memory. He promised he would do all he could for me in the future.

Within a matter of a couple of weeks, Larry Scullin retired and there were two new pairs of hands on the wheel. Tony Isaacs was the new chief and Eric Lowe was made his deputy, an arrangement I was more than pleased with. Tony had been my boss at Birkenhead and although he had a completely different personality to Richard, I found him just as easy to work for.

On his first day in charge he called me in and we chatted in general about the current drug scene.

"We know each other well, Mike," he said, "and I just want you to carry on running the squad the way you have. You have my full support." He was aware that I could ask to go back to the Birkenhead section, but I was happy to stay. "As long as I'm sitting in this chair, Mike, the job is yours. As far as I'm concerned, it's your squad."

I spent the best part of the rest of that afternoon talking to Eric, giving details of the particular operations that were up and running at the time. Eric had never before been involved in policing of this nature and he asked me how my relationship with Larry had operated.

"Basically, sir, we worked on a 'need to know' basis."

"What do you mean?"

"Well, if I felt something should be known to Larry, I would tell him straight away. If I thought he might be better not knowing, I didn't tell him at all."

"Explain."

"Yes, sir. If there was something happening that I felt Larry would approve of, but would maybe find difficult to talk about if questioned, then I didn't tell him. That way, if he were asked, he could honestly say he knew nothing about it."

"Sounds like an excellent arrangement to me. Who thought of it?"

"I did, sir."

"I bet you did, too!" Eric was quietly chuckling. "Alright, Mike, if I can't trust you, we're not going to last very long together. You tell me what you think I need to know." About a week later, I was having a coffee in the officer's mess with Eric and through the window we watched several squad members clambering into the back of a borrowed van.

"Where are they off to?" Eric asked.

"Who's that then, sir?" I replied.

"Those men of yours. And that van. Where the hell did that thing come from?"

"Sorry, Sir, I can't see a thing." He looked at me for a few seconds as if I was mad and then he smiled.

"Ah! Need to know basis. I suppose I never saw anything either." That was the start of a very amicable working relationship. Doing the work the squad was involved in, the full support and assistance of my immediate superior officers was essential. With Tony and Eric, as with Richard and Larry, I had it.

26

At twenty minutes past noon on Saturday, 2nd August 1986, a discovery was made in Birkenhead that was to push the problems of drugs into the background for many weeks. A woman was walking her dog along Borough Road, in the town centre of Birkenhead, when she discovered the near naked body of a young woman at the edge of an alleyway. Hysterical, she ran for help and the first officer on the scene was young Phil Leach. He had been with my squad but having done his stint was back in uniform.

He had arrived in response to a radio message and when I spoke to him a few days later, he was still badly shaken by the experience. The body had been found at the rubble-strewn entrance to a back alleyway. She lay in a pool of congealed blood coming from a serious head wound. Her handbag and some of her clothing was missing.

She was soon identified as twenty-one-year-old Diane Sindall, an attractive, happy-go-lucky girl with a bubbly personality. She was a much-loved daughter of a close-knit family, being one of four children. They were devastated by the news of her murder.

She was engaged to a man she had known since their schooldays and in order to save up for her forthcoming marriage she had taken up an extra job. As well as running her own florist shop by day, she was also working in the Wellington Arms pub in Bebington of an evening. She did this despite some mornings having to be up at four to purchase flowers from the wholesale market garden. The town was stunned by the brutal killing of such a popular and respectable girl and many women were to be found openly weeping in the street.

Almost immediately a massive murder hunt was mounted. Because of the ferocity and sexual nature of the attack there was a very real fear that this demented assailant might strike again. With the entire squad, I was told to drop all on-going operations and join the murder hunt. Drugs and dealers would have to take second place for a time.

The force put in a great deal of effort from the start. Fourteen hour working days became the norm and days off were usually given up. The public, for their part, gave every possible assistance. This person was wanted by everyone.

To the uninitiated, a murder control room can seem chaotic with computers flashing away, people dashing about, telephones constantly ringing and a general sense of urgency pervading every metre of space. In fact, everybody knows exactly what they are doing and what their job is.

Initial enquiries revealed that on the night she was murdered, Diane had left the Wellington Arms as usual and set off home in her car. She had been seen by two workmen leaving her car outside a tyre centre around midnight some two hundred yards from where her body was found. It was later confirmed that her car had run out of petrol and she may have been making her way to a nearby garage.

Borough Road is one of the busiest in Birkenhead, well-lit and, even at that time of night, would be busy with traffic as people made their way to and from the many night-clubs in the area. As a result of the publicity surrounding the murder, a seventeen-year-old girl came forward and reported that she had been the victim of an indecent assault shortly before and near to where Diane had left her car. She had argued with her boyfriend and was crying when she was approached by a young man who, after making some crude suggestions, sexually assaulted her before running off.

We were obviously very keen to talk to this character and two of my squad members, Frank

Thomas and Al Rushton, were engaged in this part of the enquiry. They were asking questions in a local pub where a barmaid told them a story that needed to be followed up. On the night of the murder a man had been making a nuisance of himself in the bar by making lewd and offensive suggestions to both herself and other women in the pub. This was a tough pub and he was soon put in his place, warned that if he couldn't behave he'd be thrown out.

After the pub had closed, the barmaid left and was met outside by the same man who started to walk with her. She took the first opportunity to run away from him and when she last saw him he was walking down Argyle Street South and in the direction of where the indecent assault took place.

Within four days of the murder, Frank and Al brought in a twenty-three-year-old man, Wally Rimmer, on suspicion of, at least, the assault. His home was searched and a number of items of female underwear were found for which he could offer no explanation.

Although I was aware of his detention, I had taken no part in his interrogation. Just after seven o'clock that evening though, Frank and Al came to see me.

"Boss, we know he done the assault," Al said, "but he's not having it."

"We're going to have to bail him forty-seven

three", Frank said, which meant he would be released on his own bail to return to the station and report on a specified date. "We'll put him on an identity parade in front of the girl, but we thought you might have a word with him and see what you think. We know it's him, but he's just blankin' us." They were obviously reluctant to let him go as that would allow him time to form an alibi. I wasn't short of things to do, but I had a lot of respect for the two detectives. I shrugged my shoulders and stood up.

"OK, I'll see him now, but what makes you sure he's your man?"

"When you talk to him, Boss," Frank answered, "you can just tell. Trust us, wait till you see him." I did trust them and I made my mind up to watch this man very closely while I was talking to him. He turned out to be a slim, but spotty young man who nervously wrung his hands together.

I introduced myself to him, cautioned him that he didn't have to say anything and then chatted about his background and interests. He wouldn't look me in the eye and after a few minutes I challenged him beyond what he was expecting.

"Listen, you and I know both know you did the assault." He didn't reply and looked away. "Wally, you may have done the murder, I'm not sure about that yet, but you attacked the girl in Argyle Street South. Mr Thomas knows it and Mr Rushton knows it. So, you're not going anywhere until I find out exactly what it is you've been up to. Right?" There was a brief pause and then it came out.

"I did the girl by Central station, but I never murdered anyone!" I sat back and looked at him closely and quite calmly, but inside my emotions were raging. Was I looking at the man who had so brutally murdered young Diane Sindall? I was far from convinced that I wasn't. I called Frank and Al back into the room and he repeated his confession. I take no credit for his confession, it is all swings and roundabouts. Sometimes a new face and a different style can push a suspect over the edge.

Just after eight o'clock we took him in a police vehicle to where the assault had taken place and he pointed out the spot without any assistance. He was taken back to the station and interviewed on tape.

As the assault had taken place so close to the site of the murder and at a similar time, he was clearly our prime suspect. The fact that he had demonstrated and admitted deviant sexual behaviour only reinforced the suspicion that he was the man we were looking for. Roger Corker, the superintendent in charge of the enquiry, was obviously delighted by this development, but he wasn't sitting back on his laurels.

"Right, now the hard work starts. I want him cleared or charged. I want this sorted one way or the other as soon as possible. If he's not our man, then the man we want is still walking the streets." At that stage, though, it looked very promising.

On his first appearance in court, we asked for what is known as a 'three day lie-down'. This meant that rather than being transferred to Risley Remand Centre for a week, he was held locally for three days where he could be intensely questioned.

Over those next three days, there started a series of interviews in the presence of his solicitor, Tony Nelson. Rimmer was inconsistent in his answers and must have been frustrating to his solicitor to listen as he was for us. At no time did he offer an alibi.

I conducted all of Rimmer's interviews and the final one was held in the presence of an inspector who had not sat in before. I felt I knew Rimmer quite well by now and I didn't like what I saw. A regular trick he pulled was to follow a girl home and return later to steal underwear from her washing line. He would use these for his sexual fantasies.

He was an unpleasant looking individual but boasted of numerous sexual conquests. He saw himself as a ladies man, with a perverse obsession with sexual violence. He also had an inclination for homosexual liaisons and he had no reservations in describing his male partners and their activities together.

As this particularly unpleasant interview was drawing to a close, the inspector present, shaking his head, adressed Rimmer directly.

"How do you explain these perversions to yourself?" At this, Rimmer flipped and turned to Tony Nelson.

"Who the fuck is he calling a pervert? I want to fuckin' sue him!" Tony just put his head in his hands. He then went on to finally tell us that at the time of the murder he was in a night club and gave us the names of several people who could comfirm it. They were all questioned and confirmed that at the time Diane was being murdered, he was in the club. The alibi was cast iron. He was not the murderer.

27

We were naturally disappointed by the sudden appearance of Rimmer's provable alibi, but I had long ago learned that nothing can be taken for granted in a murder hunt. We did not have all our eggs in one basket and though this had been a very promising lead it was only one of several.

After a while, it became apparent this was a marathon and not a sprint race. I had interviewed many suspects and even more potential witnesses. The total number of people spoken to by the entire murder squad ran into hundreds. Although court appearances had to continue, work on the drug scene stopped altogether and my home became a place I saw every now and again. Finally, we were put on twelve hour, nine till nine shifts.

One night, Paul Healey, who had spent the day fruitlessly following leads, came into my office and sat on the desk.

"You've worked on cases like this before, Boss," he said, "what kind of an animal can do something like this to a young girl?"

"He's not an animal, Paul, animals kill for food. This bastard killed for an evil lust, for his own demented pleasure. Come on, you've had enough for one day. I'll take you for a pint."

We looked at previously reported indecent attacks, and some unreported ones, and we were at full stretch. What was really disturbing was the number of unreported molesters freely walking around. I was too long in the job to over-react to any statistics that surfaced, but I began to genuinely fear for the female members of my family. We were living in a very unstable environment.

We received a report that a man working on the railway had found some articles on his way home from work. He would have finished work shortly before the time of the murder and as he hadn't volunteered this information himself we decided to bring him in. He turned out to be a rather pathetic individual who had invented the story to attract some attention, but the fact remained that he had been in the area at the time of the murder and so was a suspect. He was, however, in uniform and not one report had been received of anybody being seen near the scene in anything other than civilian clothes. I interviewed him and was completely satisfied he was of no interest to us.

Ray Connor, a detective chief inspector who I had worked with on the Serious Crime Squad, listened to what I had to say, but decided he would talk to him before he was released. He is a big, bluff man and as he entered the interview room the man was in the company of a young detective.

"Right, then!" he boomed across the room, "I'm making enquiries into a murder!" Before another word was spoken, the most foul smell emamated from the suspect who had literally relieved his bowels where he sat. As we all fought the instinct to throw up, Ray turned to the young officer present. "Go and get him cleaned up and send him home." Well, we'd all been young detectives at one time.

I'm not ashamed to say that during the course of the investigation I went alone to the spot where Diane had been killed. I'm not a particularly religious man, but I said a quiet prayer for her. Even now, more than ten years later, I cannot pass down that part of Borough Road, as I have done hundreds of times, without thinking of Diane.

The case was shown on BBC's *Crimewatch* and property stolen from Diane and found on Bidston Hill, a nearby beauty spot, was displayed. The items were burnt as the murderer had attempted to destroy them by setting them alight. After the programme was broadcast, a couple who had moved from Birkenhead came forward and said they had a seen a man close to the site of the fire on the same day. What they thought was particularly relevant was that they knew the man was from Birkenhead, having seen him playing darts several times in a pub in the town. They believed his name was Peter or Pat and that he had a large nose. They gave us the name of the pub in question, but although we were onto it straight away, initial enquiries failed to trace the man.

At five to eight on Monday evening, 22nd September, in the eighth week of the murder hunt, one of my lads, Craig Thompson, walked into a pub called the Old English Gentleman in Cleveland Street, Birkenhead. As he took his drink, he noticed a man who loosely fitted the description of the person we were looking for. He was watching a game of darts and without forcing the issue, Craig began to draw him into conversation. He introduced himself as Pete.

Making the excuse of visiting the toilet, Craig got to a telephone and rang in to the murder control room. I made my way down there with Jim Byrne, a detective sergeant, and after making contact with Craig, we took the man outside. He gave his name as Peter Hughes, but Craig was certain he had dealt with this man previously when using the name of Sullivan.

We stayed with him while Craig went off to check the address in nearby Queensbury

Gardens he had given us. When he came back, a neighbour had confirmed that a man by the name of Hughes and fitting his description lived there. Enquiries continued and as a result it was discovered he was using both names. He had already been interviewed once as part of the general enquiry.

In the morning, he was formally arrested and after several interviews, gave a forensic impression of his teeth. An odontologist confirmed that the bite marks on Diane's body were made by Sullivan, which turned out to be his real name. I was later called to the Queen Elizabeth II Crown Court in Liverpool to give evidence in what was to be my last murder enquiry. Hughes was convicted and given life imprisonment.

Some time later, a monument was erected on the murder spot in memory of Diane. The inscription read:

DIANE SINDALL
Murdered 2.8.1986
Because she was a woman
In memory of all our sisters
who have been raped and murdered
We will never let it be forgotten

I know of no other such memorial on Merseyside and whenever I pass it I notice that there are always fresh flowers laid there. I have no idea who leaves them.

I never knew you in life, Diane, but you touched my heart after you had gone. Rest in peace.

28

After the trial, I went abroad with Carol for a two week break and came back sure in the knowledge there was a lot of work to be done. The drug scene had been left to its own devices for nearly three months and the dealers had been making hay while the sun shone.

Merson was due in the Crown Court on the charges of supplying drugs. Mike Wolfe was for the Crown and Mercer was to be defended by a female barrister we had encountered before. He pleaded guilty to three counts, supplying heroin, possessing the same with intent to supply and possessing cannabis.

On these counts he was given four years. I was surprised at the little trouble we had had with this, bearing in mind his attitude on being arrested, but there were other more serious charges to be answered.

Four months later, the next part of the trials concerned the counts of aggravated burglary and robbery. Due to being told that a vital prosecution witness was unreliable, I made a report to both the defence and prosecution counsels and subsequently the case for those charges collapsed. I was commended by the trial judge, His Honour Mr Justice Temple, the Recorder of Liverpool, but I was only doing my duty to the courts.

A few weeks later, the next trial, which related to the 'Section 18' wounding of Ellis, began. So severe were Ellis' injuries that he had no memory of the attack. He'd told Arthur that he had been selling cannabis for Merson for about six months and that he had owed him about £250 when Merson had been arrested. Shortly after his escape, Ellis received a note from another man asking him for this cash. He could think of no other reason for Merson wanting to attack him. He also confirmed that Merson had approached him for his girlfriend's birth certificate with a view to obtaining a passport.

I was later told that Tate herself gave her evidence well and showed great courage when identifying Merson in court. The entire case could have hinged on her evidence as she was the only person who had seen Merson entering the flat just prior to the attack on Ellis. She had to go through a hell of a lot, and sadly, because of something she said, there had to be a re-trial and she had to go through it all again.

The trial was a complex one. All in all, I thought the case held together well and when the jury came back they returned a guilty verdict. Merson then pleaded guilty to assault causing actual bodily harm, possessing a loaded sawn-off shotgun and being 'unlawfully at large'.

Before passing sentence, Judge Wickham was clear in his condemnation of the convicted man.

"This was a vicious attack causing horrible injuries on a man in his own home. It was almost certainly a revenge attack because of unpaid debts. It was premeditated, planned and ruthlessly carried out." He was given ten years, which would run consecutive to the four he had already received, a total of fourteen years. A dangerous man had been taken off the streets for a long time, but I still hadn't heard the last of him.

It was at this time that we began to hear stories that police officers from an outside force were making enquiries about myself and my squad. This was soon supported by their visits to the local stations and the siezure of files relating to our enquiries. It made for an unpleasant atmosphere when they were around, but there was nothing we could do about it.

There was also a noticeable change on the street as a lot more addicts were now injecting rather than smoking heroin. To inject means that the 'buzz' they sought could be achieved more rapidly. We saw few syringes in the early days, but they were becoming more commonplace than foils and snorting tubes. This was an additional concern for the squad members as infection was a very real possibility with discarded syringes, especially now that AIDS had recently arrived on the scene. Another development had been in the emergence of organised groups of dealers. In the period between the arrests of Burley and Miller and the murder of Diane Sindall, we had been dealing largely with individuals supplying on the streets and obtaining their drugs from wherever they could. They had, however, used our absence well and small but well organised groups had been set up. We needed to get to work on this very quickly or we would soon be back to where we were when we started out two years earlier.

A brother and sister had had the cheek to start up dealing in a flat in Ford Way, a stone's throw from Upton Police Station. Steve Williams got onto them through an informant and we were able to set up our observation post in the first floor CID office of the station. We knew that a man made a regular run each evening to Liverpool for the purpose of purchasing drugs. We were in position and watching when he returned to the flat just after seven in the evening.

I left the station with Mark Gerrard, known to the lads as 'Hedgy', and we sat outside in his car waiting for the man to come out. When he did so, he got back into his own car and moved off in the direction of the Kingsway Mersey Tunnel in Wallasey. We watched him drive into the 'pipe' and decided then that money had been collected and the drop was on. We made our way back to the flat.

We forced our way into the rear of the flat and found inside fair amounts of drugs and cash. The brother and sister were both present and it was fairly obvious from the cutting gear around that they were awaiting a substantial delivery. We settled down to await the return of the man from Liverpool.

An hour later we heard and then saw him approaching the house. He looked anxious as he locked his car and was behaving very nervously as he came down the path. Whether he heard or saw something, was missing a pre-arranged all clear signal or he just had a sixth sense feeling something was wrong, I don't know. However, just as he approached the door, he suddenly turned, threw the package to the floor and ran off. As he ran, he was looking back at the building from over his shoulder which prevented him seeing Ron Hankey and Graham Clarke walking towards him. After running straight into them, which with those two must have been like running into a brick wall, he was arrested following a short scuffle. The package, containing a large quantity of heroin, was picked up and brought back into the house. When they finally went to court they received sentences of between two-and-a-half to four years.

29

Given the change in the *modus operandi* of the dealers, I believed that operational observations were the best way forward. It meant that the daily arrest count would be reduced but we were after quality rather than quantity. I discussed this with Tony and he agreed. The first planned operation of this kind was called Operation Dial-a-Smack.

It might not have been the best name thought of for an operational tag, but it was better than one the lads had come up with a short time earlier. They had been watching the activities between two houses in the same road and had called the investigation 'Operation Overture'.

"What have you called it that for?" I asked them.

"Well," one of the lads volunteered with an intelligent look on his face, "one of the houses is number 18 and the other one is number 10."

"That's very clever that, lads," I told them, shaking my head, "but I think you'll find Tchaikovsky called it the *1812 Overture*." Not great lovers of the arts were my lads.

For 'Operation Dial-a-Smack' I allocated the officers to be under the direction of sergeants Derek Bebbington and Peter Horn. It was a lot of manpower but it was needed as our information was fairly sparse.

A name we had heard of before came into the frame from the information we had received. Stan Simpson had been sent to prison about a year earlier for dealing and on his release he'd gone straight back to his old tricks. In January we'd been tipped off he was making a drop to a local prostitute and we had waited for him in the Asda car park in the town centre.

Ian Beaumont and Peter Blythe had approached his car when he turned up and identified themselves. Simpson immediately threw the car into reverse and knocked Ian to the ground. By the time we got him to stop, his female passenger and the goods had disappeared. Ian was very lucky not to have been killed or to have sustained serious injury. Simpson was charged with causing 'actual bodily harm' which was later dropped by a weak prosecution counsel. It was his personal opinion that it could not be proven that Simpson knew Ian was a policeman when he was approached. This despite him being shown their warrant cards prior to his reckless driving!

He was back on the scene and we knew we were dealing with a man who would not hesitate to use violent means to protect his business. The idea of using mobile phones to organise drug deliveries was at the time innovative and created for us a new set of problems. Orders were rung in and were followed by a return call when details of time and place of delivery would be given. This was 'mobile' business in the truest sense of the word. No names were ever used and Simpson would have to spend very little time with the drugs actually in his possession. We knew that had we raided the address to which the mobile phone was linked, we would find nothing.

After a great deal of leg-work we began to narrow down most of the activity to two houses, one in St Paul's Road and the other in Chepstow Avenue, both in Wallasey. Once Derek and Peter had secured acceptable observation points the investigation began in earnest.

Our information led us to believe that Simpson would call at the Chepstow Avenue house each evening to collect the list of orders to be dealt with that night. We soon found that he usually called around nine o'clock.

We knew that he would not be carrying, but to push the enquiry forward we made a move on him on 22nd July. We forced entry into the house after watching him enter with another man and altogether one woman and four men, including Simpson, were arrested. On his possession we found what can only be described as a long shopping list. It gave details of names, amounts and the current price list.

Precious little heroin was found and when the homes of all those arrested were searched the result was the same. Interviews back at Wallasey Station commenced but little further was revealed. The only exception was the man who had escorted Simpson into the house. He was prepared to admit he was intending to buy heroin for his own use. The prisoners were lodged overnight and after a long day I was ready for home. As I was preparing to leave, I was approached by Martin Colton who said he thought it might be worth giving Simpson's escort another chat.

"I can't put my finger on it, Boss," he said, "but I think there's more to come from him." I knew enough about my own instincts to ever ignore the gut feeling of another officer. Martin knew what he was about so, after ushering the rest of the team off to a well-earned rest, I agreed to join him.

The man concerned was John Brittain, predictably known as 'Brit' in Wallasey. As we began to question him he suddenly produced a large amount of heroin from his pocket. As he had been thoroughly searched, we were both taken aback. Apparently, he had carried the gear wrapped in a plastic bag and swallowed it when he was arrested. Once in the cells he had regurgitated the bag which many experienced couriers were trained to do. After being interviewed he took us to a house not previously known to us and there we found a quantity of documentary and physical evidence of serious dealing.

We left Simpson until the morning but it was a pleasure to talk to him. As the interview progressed the confidence slowly drained from his face and the evidence that piled up was worth the long hours we had put in. Like all other dealers, Simpson had no regard for the damage his trade caused and believed he had come up with a fool-proof plan to evade discovery. I had no sympathy for the man. The daughter of one of my informants had slashed her wrists in a desperate attempt to be free of the evil he supplied her with. I was more than pleased to see him go down for six years.

At the trial the squad was commended by the trial judge. "I praise Inspector Mulloy and his team for removing a telephone drugs link from circulation. It is realised that as rapidly as one weed is cut down another grows in its place. But the courts will do all in their powers to protect the people from the horror of heroin."

It was noticeable by this time that the bad press

was going to Liverpool. For two years we had been getting our fair share of positive publicity both in the local and national papers and on television.

30

Among the many officers I wrote up for commendation over that latest operation was a police dog-handler. He had sat alongside us with his friendly 'mutt' in cramped conditions and little in the way of food and drink. It was never pleasant work, but the officer had co-operated in all aspects of the work and for the duration of the operation was very much part of the squad.

I was surprised when I received a call from his superintendent asking me whether he really deserved such recognition. Considering it was a reflection on his command, I could not fathom why he wouldn't be delighted. Such commendations must have been fairly few and far between. Throughout my service, dogs and their handlers were always ready to assist at any hour of the day and night. The animals would be used as guard dogs or sniffer dogs. My ambition when

I first joined the job was to be a dog-handler and, although I eventually went down a different road, I always appreciated their worth. This was reciprocated when I retired with a card of congratulations coming from their section.

Arthur at one time applied to join the dog section and I was happy to write him up for the post. He was sent for by Richard and he enjoyed a fun-filled twenty minutes with his deputy Larry at Arthur's expense.

"They don't have a collar to fit you, Arthur," said Richard.

"And we can't find a handler who's prepared to take you on," added Larry.

"The accommodation is adequate, but you might find the food a little disagreeable." The pair of them were thoroughly enjoying themselves and were close to hysterics. Eventually, Richard took a deep breath and ripped up the request in front of a subdued Arthur. "Get out of here, Cowley, and lock somebody up." As Arthur made his way out of the office, he stopped at the door and turned to Richard.

"Does this mean I'm not getting it then, Boss?"

I knew by now that it was the West Yorkshire Police who were leading the enquiry into the squad. We were seeing them frequently in the area and at local stations, but neither I nor any members of the squad were appproached officially. They had though spoken to many people we had dealings with, including informants. I accepted that this kind of enquiry has to take place from time to time and somebody has to do it. I felt, though, that there is a proper way to do it.

A superintendent and an inspector called on one of my female informants and spoke to her in the company of her mother. She was told she had to make a statement, but replied that she would rather talk to me first.

"I'm afraid you have no choice in the matter," said the superintendent, quite brusquely. He was about to encounter the wrath of a Scouse mother for the first time.

"Oh, doesn't she? Do you have a warrant?"

"Er . . . no."

"Well, fuck off then and don't come back without one!"

"Excuse me, there's no need . . ."

"Go on! You heard me! Fuck off!" Not much later I was asked to approach the woman and, approached in the right way with due respect given, both she and her daughter were happy to help in any way they could.

I was told by my chief superintendent that the BBC were making a programme and that on the chief constable's orders, I was to fully cooperate. I wasn't that enamoured by the idea but had no choice but to go along with it. I met with the programme producer and with his team he followed us around for a few days. During the course of their presence, we busted a house in Wallasey on the strength of information received by Geoff Higgs and a few weeks later, the morning after the documentary had been broadcast, I was summoned by the duty inspector who told me the arrested man had made a complaint. He was not happy about the incident being televised, although his face had never been shown.

"As you know," the chief superintendent said, "I have to submit a report and I need to know who was responsible for the raid to be able to complete the form."

"Chief Constable Ken Oxford," I told him, "we were working to his orders." I don't think he had the bottle to write that down. In any case, I heard nothing more about it.

I was out having a drink with Carol one evening in a pleasant little pub near Heswall when I was confronted by a drug supplier I'd been responsible for sending to prison a while back. What seemed at first to be a potentially unpleasant situation never materialised and I was invited with Carol to a house party to celebrate the dealer's release from prison earlier that day. I had a drink with him and his boisterous family and group of friends but declined the invitation. The mind boggles at how that might have gone once everyone was the worse for a few drinks.

With the reduction in the squad's numbers, we were never going to be as effective as we had been, but there was still a lot for us to do. The next investigation was Operation Brynmoss, led by Steve Williams, Mike McDonough and Dave McGarvie. The Brynmoss was a small estate in Rock Ferry and we had been receiving more and more information regarding a nest of dealers. What had only recently been a peaceful and problem-free area was now swarming with addicts and dealers. Various men, living on the estate at different addresses, had combined to form a sizeable operation. The heroin was coming from Liverpool and unknown couriers were coming from outside the area also. The dealing was taking place both from flats and on the street.

One lad involved was known as 'Dykey Dave', so called because of the drugs he had been legally prescribed. One day each week he was the most popular man in the area. When he received his weekly prescribed drugs he would give away what gear he was carrying free of charge because he was so stoned.

During the course of the enquiry we heard of an armed man coming over from Liverpool to settle a dispute. On another occasion a uniformed officer was threatened by a man carrying a gun in the early hours of the morning. This was taken very seriously by Tony, the chief superintendent, and Operation Brynmoss became the largest operation of its kind ever set up on the Wirral.

After a painstaking period of observation and questioning, we found that the family largely responsible was the Finch family, well known to officers on the north bank of the Mersey. The mother, Irene, and her husband, Henry, had both recently served three years for drug supply, but had immediately recommenced business on their release.

Irene Finch was organising distribution from several flats and on the streets and it was soon apparent that business was being conducted as openly as if it were candy-floss they were selling.

I had officers posing as street-cleaners, council workmen and deliverymen and we soon had an enormous amount of detail to work from. Finally, on 9th December 1987, I led a team to hit the Finch residence.

Di Ethelstone approached Irene Finch and asked her directly if she had illegal substances in her possession. After some fidgeting, she produced several ounces of wrapped heroin she had concealed within her vagina. Di's disgust at this revelation was coupled with the relief that she had not been forced to conduct a body search. Cash and stolen property were also recovered and both Irene and Henry Finch were arrested and charged with possession with intent to supply.

The following day we smashed our way into several flats in the area and actually caught red-handed one man, Anthony Glass, cutting his deals. Another woman, Ann Williams, was arrested in the neighbouring flat. She admitted dealing, but would provide no further information. There was a shotgun in circulation and she was terrified of having her head blown off, she told us.

While we there a man called at her flat wearing overalls. She tried to help him out.

"Have you come to fix the boiler?" she said.

"Er . . . yeah, that's right. Where is it?"

"Give it up, son," I said, taking him by the arm, "how long have 'Terry's Auto Repairs' been fixing boilers?" He admitted to buying heroin on a regular basis from Williams and had told his employers he was test driving a customer's car. I've no idea how he explained an absence of more than four hours.

We made a number of arrests but had not been able to obtain the name of the Liverpool supplier, but our luck soon changed. We heard that Glass' wife had continued to deal after her husband's arrest so we paid her a visit. We found her in the company of another man busy cutting up deals. As we were recovering a large amount of heroin from underneath a child's cot, the man threw himself through the living room window and limped off as quickly as he could. I got on the radio to Stan Preston, working with me for the first time since we were together on my uniformed section at Birkenhead, and he was picked up a few minutes later when he turned up in a taxi outside another flat we were watching.

I was a bit peeved when Finch and her husband both succeeded in obtaining bail, but I was consoled by the knowledge that they would deal again straight away, which they did.

I was contacted by Finch, who offered me information on drug related matters. She told us that a friend of hers, Joan Little, could give us details on a man who was coming over from Liverpool to obtain substantial amounts of heroin. Little was a major Liverpool dealer who was at the time on bail charged with dealing.

She arranged to ring later, but my suspicions were roused and the call was taped. Finch said she was ringing from Little's home and that she had heard a rumour that money had gone missing after a raid on a dealer. She then asked to speak to me.

"I've heard a lot about you, Mr Mulloy." Although nothing of any substance was said, I was now convinced we were being set up and instructed my officers to have nothing to do with either of them. We had found that it was, in fact, Little who was supplying Finch, but I could only guess at what their game was. On 8th January, I found out.

31

A number of warrants had been issued for the Brynmoss and Finch and her husband were once again in possession of large amounts of heroin and once again arrested. Finch this time broke down and admitted to supplying on a major scale on behalf of Little.

The following day, Stan took a team to Little's home and she was arrested. It was a job that required skilful handling and Stan, on his first raid with the squad, did a splendid job. I hadn't seen much of Stan since the night we were chasing house-burglars through Birkenhead Park, and I had specificly requested he be transferred to the squad. Stan had worked hard for his rank and expected to be properly addressed. In the squad, however, such formalities were often dropped as it would be ridiculous to refer to each other as 'sir', 'boss' or 'sarge' when in public. I explained this to Stan and he was quite happy about it. Hedgy had been a recruit with Stan and knowing he was usually such a stickler for formality couldn't resist it.

"Well, are you gettin' the teas in, Stan?"

"Don't push it, Mark," I warned him.

Little was brought to Wallasey and let us know she had been told by a Liverpool superintendent, who she named, never to talk to officers from Wirral. She was soon put right about that and afterwards 'rolled over'. After her interview, I was with Di in the interview room when Little was dealing with the numerous forms that had to completed. Di asked her when she had last worked.

"Well, I used to be on the game," she said, "but it was dead fuckin' borin'."

Rumours were rife about her having numerous 'friends' and contacts, but whoever they were, they did her no good and she was sent down for seven years. It was estimated that her team had shifted just over £594,000 worth of heroin in just a few months. Altogether, fourteen people received prison sentences and the squad were again praised by the presiding judge when passing sentence.

"This is the end of a serious case involving large numbers of persons in the Rock Ferry area of Birkenhead, in the supply of heroin in the Brynmoss area. A tremendous amount of work has gone on in this case by Inspector Mulloy and his officers. They are to be congratulated and commended."

My old friend James Wren had resurfaced and was once again working the area around Bedford Road. Rock Ferry was being reduced to an open drug market and it was taking up as much of our time as Lynmouth Gardens had once. We found that addicts could buy heroin on two corners, cannabis on another and amphetamines on a fourth. This looked straightforward enough, but it would involve a lot of men. Tony, an ex-CID man, was fully supportive of the way we were going about things. We didn't take long to decide to go for it.

We had learned from previous operations such as Brynmoss that photographs had their limitations as they could be interpreted in so many different ways. Although video surveillance had not been used before on drug operations, I thought it would be ideal for our needs. Apart from the broader impact of what was being televised, it also automatically recorded the precise time and date that those events were taking place.

Tony agreed to both the use of videos and the numbers I had suggested were required. It was at times like this that I appreciated having a senior officer who saw the job as I did. We set up in Bedford Road and Medway Road, where Wren lived close by on the other side of the railway bridge. We soon found that Wren hardly ever moved from his home these days. His dealers would call and drop off cash, have the drugs they had sold replaced and would return to the 'marketplace'.

Everything was very transparent and on tape. Steve Williams, Ron Hankey and Sybil Hardacre did a first-class job on the Bedford Road post and I take my hat off to Hedgy, Graham Clarke and Mark Wilson in Medway Road. In order to watch Wren they had to arrive at their post, the attic of a derelict house, just after dawn and then stay there until it was dark. They had no facilities for refreshments, no toilet facilities and the constant company of rats. It was excellent and dedicated police work and they all deserved the position of team leader for their efforts when the doors went in.

Wren, it appeared, only trusted the dealers with so much at a time. He was determined and dangerous, a point reinforced by the information we received that he now had access to firearms. A female informant had named Wren as the supplier of heroin while another man was responsible for the cannabis and amphetamines. She was able to give us considerable details on the personalities involved.

I had never known so many dealers to be working from the same location, but they were, according to our source, confident that the location gave them security. The videos were shown to local officers and slowly real names and addresses were put to the nicknames, such as 'Pretty Boy', we provided. Watching more closely, we could see that dealers were not selling to anybody they didn't know personally unless they were first introduced by somebody they did. The deals went on in sun, wind and rain and customers came and went on foot, bikes and in cars. The whole thing was taking place so smoothly, ordinary members of the public were passing by oblivious to what was going on.

The dealing went on from early morning to late at night. Dealers took over from each other. We saw one juvenile buying heroin and then immediately re-selling the drug to his friends of the same age. As I watched the scene over a period of a few days it was difficult to take in. Even though I had become hardened to the scale and nature of drug activity over the previous couple of years, I still found all this breathtaking. The numbers of people, buying and selling, was well in excess of a hundred and completely beyond anything we had tackled before.

The logistics involved in an operation of this size were considerable, and I spent a long time with Tony going over everything. First, we agreed that all those arrested should be held at Bromborough Police Station. This was out of the way and the night before we intended to close the 'market', Tony rang the station's duty inspector to let him know he would have his hands full the following day. He added that security was paramount and that he should tell only those people who had to know. It would be frustrating beyond words to have the whole thing ruined by one idle comment to the wrong ears.

The problems of manpower and transport were agreed and then the detail of how the operation would unfold was gone into. The importance of not talking was also drilled into the squad. When we were about to arrest Miller, two bobbies, not even involved in the enquiry, told a barmaid that Miller was due to be picked up. It turned out the barmaid was his niece.

A new superintendent had taken over the Drug Squad and I was pleased to hear he was keen to build bridges. He let me know that the assistant chief constable for crime was asking why his squad were not receiving the same favourable reports in the press as the Wirral Crime Squad. The superintendent concerned was happy to send over manpower and cover overtime, but his lads got a flea in their ear from mine when they wandered about talking to addicts and probing them.

It was on 12th May 1988 at six o'clock in the morning when seventy officers assembled at Bromborough Police Station. Apart from my own lads there were Drug Squad, Special Branch and uniformed officers present. At seven o'clock we started knocking doors in.

As the prisoners began to flood in, it was initially chaotic. In his conscientious efforts to maintain security, the Bromborough inspector had told nobody at all about the imminent explosion in activity so consequently the station was taken totally by surprise at this sudden invasion. There was just one custody officer to book everybody in and we had the facility of just one interview room. The canteen was wiped out of its stores within two hours of our getting there.

32

I set up office in the detective inspector's office with Ben, the DI being away on leave. The job was going well, with substantial amounts of drugs and cash, as well as some firearms being recovered. Once the arrests were done, there were a total of sixty-five people in custody, another record. The interviews were exceptionally productive. As each of the dealers was shown videotape of their activities, their initial claims of innocence were washed away. They had never before been confronted with the technique and had no answer to it.

As the station was filled to capacity, chaos reigned. As well as the exceptional numbers of police officers and suspects, the numbers were swelled through the day by the appearance of dozens of solicitors. We had managed to set up another two interview rooms, but the process was still very slow and as the day turned into evening we were all exhausted.

At nine o'clock I called a meeting with the solicitors present and told them there would be no more interviews until the morning. A rota system was worked out so that each solicitor could arrange for his several clients to be interviewed at approximately the same time of the day and they could come into the station and not have to waste their very valuable time waiting around.

Wren was, once again, desperate to do a deal, but I had no intention listening to him. We all set off home to snatch some sleep and the following day we somehow managed to get through the rest of the interviews.

The morning after the trial, two of my lads went over to HQ in Canning Place, Liverpool to deliver some exhibits that were to be sent to forensics and overheard a Drug Squad inspector talking to a number of officers. He was obviously unaware who they were.

"Yeah, well, Mulloy rang me a few weeks ago and said he was having a lot of trouble and was concerned about the area. I told him not to worry and sent a few lads over there to do the observations and tidy the job up for him. All he has to do is finish the file and it's all wrapped up!" He was a little perturbed when I called him later and said as he had done the rest of the job it was only fair he should finish the paperwork and asked him where I should send it.

Richard Henriques, QC, with David Steer as his junior were briefed for the Crown. I held several conferences with them and they were of inordinate help, with so many defendants, in advising schedules of the video tapes for the most professional way of presenting the case to the jury. Once again, we had nowhere else to go for advice, so it was down to us to make progress. Because of the numbers involved, a courtroom of the Queen Elizabeth II Crown Courts in Liverpool was used for the committal proceedings for the first time in its history.

Security was a problem at an ordinary magistrates' court, so Norman Draper, the deputy clerk to Wirral justices, kindly arranged, with the consent of the Lord Chancellor, to have one of the Crown courts dubbed a magistrates' court for the period of these earlier hearings.

Wren and fifteen other people pleaded guilty to charges of supplying heroin and received various custodial sentences. At their trial, His Honour Judge Arthur praised the squad.

"I would like to commend the police officers in this case. I have nothing but praise for the police in bringing the operation to a successful conclusion, accomplished with patience and skill."

Those not convicted of dealing heroin were charged with a variety of offences. It was a very satisfying operation. In a later raid, we came across a letter sent from one of the defendants while he was on remand awaiting trial. He was in a confident mood.

"I'm looking forward to getting out soon. This operation was Mulloy's biggest mistake." We all had a little chuckle at that.

I felt at this time I was becoming a little jaded. For the first time in my service I was becoming disillusioned about the whole thing. I was putting in ridiculous hours, many of which I wasn't being paid for. There was constant stress and I was always planning and preparing one thing while trying to bring something else to a close. I was constantly confronted with reams of paperwork which never seemed to diminish for long, no matter how conscientious I was in working on it. I was permanently drained and could see no purpose in it.

I still had no prospect of promotion and it was an open secret who was blocking me. When I applied for a post of chief inspector outside my own force, I was not recommended for interview. To add insult to injury, I was the subject of an investigation.

I tried for another posting outside the force, with tongue in cheek as much as anything else. Unlike my previous application, I was totally unsuitable for the job and had no relevant experience. To show just how daft it all was, I was actually put forward for it. My interview was a complete waste of time. I didn't have the remotest chance of getting the job and I'm sure the senior officers who interviewd me must have wondered what the hell I was doing there.

After talking it through with Carol I decided to put my dissatisfaction at being constantly over-looked for promotion on the record. It was never my intention to obtain anything more than a frank and honest reply. I was not interested in tribunals or any such nonsense, but I didn't have that long left in the job and was thinking that maybe I should look for a new life outside the service. I accepted that not everyone can win, but I wasn't even in the race.

At the time, I had been commended more times than any other officer in the history of my force with a total of twenty-seven up to the end of 1988. I had passed my promotion board in 1976 and again in 1982 under a new system. I noted that since my being made an inspector at Birkenhead, there had been a total of 170 promotions to chief inspector. I asked directly if there was a reason I should be made aware of that was prohibiting my chances of promotion. I gleaned a lot of satisfaction from submitting it and waited for the ripples to start.

The first came from Maurice Morrell, the chief inspector of the administration unit and an admirer of our squad. Nothing was ever too much trouble for him. He congratulated me on my submission and suggested it was somebody's turn to 'grasp the nettle'.

I didn't wait long. Tony called me and asked me to go and see him. He was fully supportive as usual but thought I should make some amendments.

"I wouldn't dispute one word you're saying here, Mike, but as it stands it will have political repercussions you don't intend. The object is to get the issue of your promotion, or lack of it, out into the open. I suggest you tone one or two parts of it down." I trusted Tony and thought he was giving me sensible advice. I made the changes.

Tony went on to tell me that I had been his first nomination for promotion for the last two years. Two days after I received a report from Assistant Chief Constable Howe asking me to make an appointment to see him. I had never met the man before, but he seemed to know all about my record. His explanation was that I must have slipped through the net in error as there seemed to be no plausible explanation for my being constantly overlooked.

I knew the truth, as I'm sure he did, but I went along with it and left his office with reassurances that I was very much in the frame for promotion. I felt I should have done something about it years ago, but better late than never. The strain of running the office got no easier. Being local officers locking up local people we were well known and much resented by many. There was a need to be constantly on guard, but in fact very little happened. I was warned by one lad we had locked up that he had overheard two dealers talking in prison about myself and Arthur, stating that if they couldn't get us, they would get our families. All this kind of thing added to the building tension.

33

The north end of Birkenhead is a throw-back in time to when community spirit meant something. It was a tough, unrelenting area of high unemployment, but was where old people were not neglected and people genuinely cared for their neighbours. It was a difficult area to police and authority was resented, but at least you always knew where you stood.

In the late seventies I had been a detective inspector with the Serious Crimes Squad and was engaged in an enquiry concerning a series of horrific rapes on or around the north end. Apart from the fear that the rapist could strike at any time, there was an increasing belief that he could resort to murder. We received enormous help from the local community and on the night the man was arrested, we were bought drinks by people who would not normally have given us the time of the day.

In the aftermath of Miller's reign there had been an attempt by a gang from Liverpool to move in on the vacant north end, but it had been very quickly nipped in the bud and chased back to where it came from.

In the end, though, there was such an alarming amount of drug trade in the area that it had become known locally as "Smack Hill". We set out to get to the root of it. Our initial enquiries seemed to indicate a number of independent suppliers, but it didn't fit the usual pattern as there was an unusual amount of reluctance to talk to us. It seemed there was a grip of fear holding the area. Even when we had seen deals taking place, it was always adamantly denied later. Observation was difficult and it was decided as people expected to see police cars from time to time, we could fairly effectively watch what was going on by quite openly driving around as if on normal patrols.

The pieces began to fit into place when I was contacted by a young woman who had proved to be a reliable informant in the past. She was very nervous at seeing me and suggested we meet in Chester. I agreed but took Bob Jones and Ron Hankey with me as a precaution. She told us that rather than being a number of independent operators the area was fiercely controlled by a man called David Patterson. He already had a serious criminal record, including four years for drug supply and seven years for armed robbery. He was a sinister figure with a reputation for extreme violence, feared amongst his own.

Nobody was dealing on the North End without his consent and she knew of several people beaten by baseball bats and iron bars and had herself been so badly beaten she had spent several days in hospital. Not surprisingly, not one of these attacks had been reported to the police.

This needed careful handling and I decided in the first place to have Ron, Hedgy and Ben O'Brien form an intelligence team. I then gave Bob Jones and his entire team of Mo Jones, Joe Danher, Frank Liston and Dave Connor the responsibility of observation and video evidence. The very nature of the north end made this a very difficult and awkward operation to handle and the first problem was to secure a satisfactory observation point. To this day, the local belief is that we used the local church steeple, an idea enhanced by the subsequent reporting in the press of the codename for the investigation: Operation Steeple.

We had considered using it, but decided against it first on some kind of moral ground, because it didn't seem right to use a church for surveillance. A more honest reason was provided by one of the lads who volunteered to go up and look around to see what it offered. He returned covered in bird shit and made everybody's mind up that we'd find somewhere else.

Even now, I cannot say where we were able to locate ourselves but it proved to be excellent for the purposes. Quite suddenly, all the deals began to take place down an alleyway almost directly opposite the observation point. When the position was first taken there had been a young tree planted directly in between, but after the first night it 'mysteriously' disappeared. When the matter was raised it was put down to 'young hooligans'.

It appeared there was an organised shift-system of dealers operating from the alleyway and, as the faces came and went, many were already familiar to us. Most of the dealers arrived at the location by taxi and stayed for about four hours before being replaced by the next dealer. A public telephone close by was used as an office and more in-coming calls were received than there were calls made. Patterson appeared at least once every day and from his body language it was clear he was keeping a supervisory eye on his own operation.

Each night, when dealing was finished for the day, we were initially intrigued by the arrival of a man who would disapppear down the alleyway for a few minutes. We passed on the video evidence to the technical unit who were able to enhance the gloomy pictures and reveal that the man was employed to clear any signs of the day's business, picking up wraps, needles, foils and even used matches. Such evidence of drug activity was regularly given to the police by angry and/or frightened local residents.

For eleven long and harrowing days the observations continued. It was bed to work and back to bed with the only respite being the occasional snatched hour in the bar in the Wallasey station. Even then, the sole topic of conversation was the progress of the investigation. I was well aware that the longer the operation went on the greater was the risk of discovery, so we had to move in soon. At the same time, if the activity was taken out cleanly and completely, it would simply move elsewhere.

As an example of the measures taken to avoid discovery, a typical transaction would involve the potential buyer being directed to the alleyway by a man standing a little distant from it. This would be Patterson if he was there. This added the additional precautionary measure of being able to vet the customer while acting as full-time lookout. The customer then approached the dealer, frequently a woman, and, in the company of a minder, they would enter the alleyway. The hidden heroin would then be produced, one female dealer had it concealed in her knickers, and the deal would take place. The minder would then lead the couple to the edge of the alleyway and wait. Shortly afterwards a man would pass them and tug on his collar, which we later deduced was an all-clear signal.

I decided now that the video evidence we had was indisputable and that there was sufficient of it to prove the volume of trade taking place. As well as observing all this activity, a great deal of work had to be done on the whereabouts of these people at any particular time of the night or day. They were never all 'on location' at the same time, but we would have to carry out all raids simultaneously. It was, therefore, vital that the information we had regarding the addresses of those involved was correct and right up to date. This is not as straightforward as it might seem. Those involved in criminal activity frequently change their address on a regular basis for the very purpose of staying one step ahead of the police.

I decided that the raids would take place in the early hours of the morning when they would all be in their beds. It was dawn on Friday, 28th October, 1988 when I drove into Wallasey station and met up with the sixty officers who would be taking part in the raids. Members of my squad were made team leaders and each was given a pack containing warrants, names of nominated officers, equipment details, information and photographs of suspects and a list of their allocated transport.

I held a conference with all the officers before they went into their own huddles to arrange their own particular tactics. Just after five thirty everybody made their way to their positions and by six everyone was in place. I was with Ben and had decided to move around the area as needs arose, but my first port-of-call was Patterson's home.

I sat in the car and looked at Ben. He had been a tower of strength in the past and, as a typical Irishman, was always abundantly optimistic. He gave me his usual confident smile.

"Well, Boss, win or lose, we're here." I collected my thoughts, picked up the hand-set and asked for the facility giving me simultaneous access to all police cars. I looked at my watch. Exactly six o'clock. Without further hesitation I gave the order.

"Strike! Strike! Strike!"

Each team leader acknowledged the order by repeating it back to me and after the word came spitting back at me a couple of dozen times, the radio was silent.

34

Within minutes the silence was shattered as a succession of animated messages were broadcast:

"Successful entry made!"

"Suspect detained!"

"Premises secured!"

"Search in progress!"

"Suspect detained!"

"Suspect detained!"

"Suspect detained!"

Ron and Hedgy had specifically requested the raid on Patterson's home and, given their overall contribution to the enquiry, it was the least they deserved. Patterson emerged from his house in their company and there was no sign of his two ferocious rotweilers. There was though a police alsation and his handler, the dog having put the two to flight as soon as the house was entered. Patterson, as with many others arrested that morning, had resisted arrest with violence, but all had been overcome. Patterson was glaring at anything that moved as he was placed into the back of a police car.

I made my way back to Wallasey to organise the reception committee and the next few hours were filled with arrested men and women being brought into the station, along with considerable hauls of drugs, cash and stolen property. The cells were quickly filling up. Throughout this period we could hear Patterson barking orders that nothing should be admitted. There was no mistaking the menace in his tone.

Despite initial denials, each of the suspects was astounded by both the quality and quantity of the video evidence shown to them. In turn, some began to capitulate. Ken Johnson and Billy Morris dealt with a man who completely broke down and asked if he could see his wife waiting outside, after which he would tell us everything. When he told her he was 'dead and buried', she started to scream and told him to tell us 'fuck all'. He was obviously more frightened of her than he was Patterson, because that's exactly what he told us.

We weren't finished with 'Smack Hill'. It would have been too much to hope that all suspects would be caught up in the first wave and that proved to be the case. Some of the officers returned to the target addresses and reports were coming in of crowds gathering around the homes of those men arrested. Some were confused customers wandering around for their supply, but the great majority were jubilant residents delighted that a scourge on their neighbourhood had been removed. The mood was up-beat and there was no shortage of wit about.

"Well, I'm not saying the people are pleased with us," one of the lads called in, "but we're gettin' invited to a lot of street parties!"

Mobile snatch squads were organised to pick-up the remaining suspects off the streets and by the time we were done and the dust settled we had forty-one people in custody being interviewed on a variety of drug-related charges.

The following night became a particularly important one for me, although I didn't know it at the time. I was at the station when a telephone call came in from one the few remaining suspects we had not yet arrested. He wanted to know why we were looking for him, but he was so high he told me where he was on the Woodchurch and agreed to wait for me to pop out and see him to clear up any misunderstanding. As everybody was up to their eyes, I made my own way to the shops in Hoole Road to pick him up. As it turned out, he was to be the last person, of so very many over the years, that I personally arrested. An officer always remembers the first and last collar he feels and I am no exception.

A great deal of preparation went into the trial cases and we were well rewarded when one defence counsel after another threw the towel in and strongly recommended to their client to plead guilty. I was denied my request to use the same prosecution team I had successfully worked with on the second Operation Bedford, but my fears were proven totally unjustified with the appointment of Mr Waldron, QC, and his assistant Mr Lewis.

Not all of those charged pleaded guilty and the ensuing trial was as difficult and bitterly fought as any other. Patterson, not surprisingly, offered the greatest resistance and his menacing presence and attempts at manipulation during the whole process was a feature of the trial. He was one angry man.

The trials lasted several weeks before His Honour Mr Justice Lachs, and four complete days were spent watching video evidence. Once the jury retired the fact that it was not cut and dried was indicated by their returning three times to view again extracts from the videos.

Eventually, they returned with their verdicts after three days of deliberations. Two of the accused on the periphery of the organisation were acquitted but seven of the nine who had not pleaded guilty were convicted on charges of supply. Patterson received eight years and two of his deputies received six each. Another two got five, one got thirty months and the common-law wife of Patterson received six months.

The judge commended the squad after sentencing.

"The police officers who have been engaged in Operation Steeple are to be commended. Some have given evidence over a long period of the time to the court. One can't help feeling, and they are justified, their satisfaction with the verdicts of the jury. What they have said has been shown to be good, honest and decent policing. Allegations made that they have behaved improperly have been dismissed by the verdicts of the jury."

I make no apology for relating the occasions when a judge praised the squad and the work they had put into an investigation. Such commendations are fairly rare and are highly regarded within the force.

I personally never felt any satisfaction at seeing men going to prison and was aware that they often left innocent wives and children to fend for themselves. It is the price they have to pay and I could muster very little sympathy for Patterson as he left the dock.

I was happy with the judge's commendation but I was more pleased with an anonymous letter from a member of the public, passed on to me via the chief constable. In it, the writer congratulated us on our work in the North End of Birkenhead and stated we should be given more leeway in our efforts to combat the problems of drugs. She offered us her profuse thanks and signed it simply 'the mother of a heroin addict'.

35

I had to step in and put a stop to one of Ben O'Brien's regular pranks. A very pleasant, but painfully shy woman worked in the administration unit and, in fairness, was somewhat in awe of my motley crew and their raucous ways. Each time Ben passed her in the corridor, he would make some comment.

"Tickle your arse with a feather!"

"I beg your pardon?"

"I said it's typical Wallasey weather!"

"Oh, yes, quite."

He did it so often to her she was considering having her ears tested.

A day or two after the trial, Ben took one of the squad's cars to the police garage for its routine service. A short while later, Tony received a complaint from the chief inspector of the traffic department about the unwashed and generally unkempt condition of the car when it arrived. His mechanics were disgusted by the number of empty Coke cans, crisp packets and chip wrappings they found on the floor and under the seats. They were also horrified to discover in the boot sledge-hammers marked 'WCS', so clearly they were ours. The complaint was passed on to me for comment. Comment I did.

I pointed out that cars in general in the area we operated were not noted for being immaculately cleaned and it was important our vehicles did not stand out. I was pleased to hear the Coke cans were not beer cans. I stated finally that I had more important matters to address than such petty complaints.

The man had foolishly booked the sledge-hammers into the property system and I was pleased to hear he was now being inundated with slips asking how he proposed to dispose of them. The squad replaced them with the co-operation of local garages and building sites within a matter of days. The public were on our side even if some sections of the force were not.

Operation Steeple was my last major investiga-tion as the squad commander. We had been under investigation for more than a year from officers of the West Yorkshire Police led by Chief Superintendent McQuoid. Although it was informants on the street who had first told us about it, we were all interviewed several times over a period of time. Officers from West Yorkshire were all over the place talking to people and seizing files, records and log books. It was now our turn to be pursued.

I was totally confident we had nothing to fear from any independent investigation, but at the same time it is not pleasant having your operations investigated by fellow officers.

They too are being monitored and therefore do a very thorough job.

The months passed and the internal enquiry rolled on. I was told confidentially that it represented the largest investigation of its kind ever carried out on a provincial force. By the time they were done, the cost to the ratepayer was well over a million pounds.

Eventually, on 1st December, I was served with the first of more than fifty disciplinary papers in respect of allegations made against me by both Merson and Burley. The vast majority related to matters that could have been raised at their respective trials, but never were. In the main they consisted of conspiracy to pervert the course of justice and the fabrication of evidence. I was quite bemused that they included an allegation that I had colluded in Merson's escape and had threatened to shoot him if he reneged on a deal I was supposed to have made with him. It was a variation on the theme of his postcard from Ringway airport.

Arthur was told over the telephone that he was to be served with forty-three discipline sheets and reacted in the way only Arthur could.

"Bloody hell," he shouted down the phone, "what about my street cred? My boss got fifty-one!"

Many other officers received similar papers and the whole thing, despite Arthur's attitude, caused a lot of anxiety for a lot of people as months passed with no further word.

Feelings were not improved by the appearance of an article on the front page of the *Liverpool Echo*.

POLICE PROBE FRAME-UP PLOT!
Mersey detectives accused of lying to
get man jailed!

The story mentioned the internal enquiry being carried out by officers of the West Yorkshire Police and revealed that they had gone to the expense of travelling to the States to interview Merson's girlfriend, although the details of the people actually making the allegations were not given.

I was informed via an interim report from the Police Complaints Authority that they were satisfied with the investigation. A staggering total of 144 statements had been taken and 339 documents submitted. I sat back and confidently awaited the outcome.

As the months again went by, I submitted several reports on behalf of several officers who were becoming concerned at the lack of urgency and apparent indifference to their welfare. Still I heard nothing.

Things were brought to a head when Detective Constable John Gardiner entered the witness box at the Crown Court to give evidence against a relative of Merson's on a totally unconnected matter.

The newspaper article was produced and shown to the jury, followed by a suggestion that his client had been arrested as part of a conspiracy to get at Merson. It was a successful ploy and the defendant was acquitted.

Enough.

I decided to take the bull by the horns and within a few days had submitted a lengthy report pulling no punches. I pointed out that morale was suffering and that certain officers and their families were under enormous strain. I stressed that I did not take the responsibilities of leadership lightly, but that officers who worked with me had come to me with what I felt was a genuine grievance. I believed that the time taken to produce the results of the enquiry would not have been tolerated in any other job outside the police force and said so.

A response came within a few days. No further action in respect of any criminal charges would be taken against any officer who was, or had been, serving with the Wirral Crime Squad. We were neither exonerated, nor publicly cleared. The whole matter was just ended after two years, thousands of man hours and a fortune in cost for this sorry conclusion to be reached. If only I had been granted such liberties with public purse-strings!

There was no redress. Criminals have nothing to lose in making wild allegations. Complaining and causing hassle is part of their game. It is no wonder some officers say 'why bother?'

One immediate consequence of this result, or lack of, was that all officers could now receive their richly deserved commendations earned in the last two years. One Monday afternoon seventeen past and present squad members assembled in the office dining room of the police HQ in Canning Place and awaited the arrival of Chief Constable Jim Sharples. He had been slightly delayed and turned up finally in the company of a very young looking superintendent serving as his staff officer.

As we were called to attention, I cringed when

Ben explained, in a voice just a little too loud, the reason for the Chief Constable's late arrival.

"It's not the Chief's fault," explained Ben without a hint of sarcasm, "he had to collect the Super from school!"

36

I was enjoying a coffee in the Wallasey station canteen with some of the lads when Hedgy appeared anxiously at the door. It was a late afternoon in early December, 1988.

"Boss! You're wanted on the phone. It's ACC Adams." He was understandably flustered. Young officers do not often get to talk with senior officers of such rank, even over the telephone.

I made my way to my deserted office and took the call.

"Are you sitting down, Mike?" Richard sounded quite cheerful.

"Of course not, sir! I'm standing rigidly to attention!"

"And quite right too," Richard chuckled. "I have some excellent news for you, Mike. You have been promoted. After Christmas you are going to Birkenhead as Chief Inspector and Deputy

Commander. My congratulations, no one deserves it more." I stuttered a thank you, but I'm not sure I made very much sense. I knew this was down to Richard. He had promised he would do what he could for me and, as usual, he had delivered.

I rang Carol immediately. It was as much her promotion as mine and was the best possible Christmas present. I had waited fifteen years to be promoted from inspector and I was elated. The squad had been a resounding success since its formation and I was proud of my part in it. We had arrested more than 2,300 prisoners and detected over 3,500 burglaries. We had recovered hundreds of thousands of pounds worth of stolen property. Richard had wanted convictions and he got them. We had smashed the syndicates and taken the investigation of drug activity onto a new level. At last, despite all that I had been through, I felt that I had received my just reward.

My promotion 'do' was held at the Birkenhead Police Club and I think that just about everyone who had been involved with the squad at some time or another turned up. There were personal friends, civilian employees and others from my time in the uniform section. I was pleased to see Tommy Hall, my sergeant from my early CID days who had taught me what being a detective was all about. I had used many of the techniques he showed me on the squad.

My old partner from the sixties and seventies, Mike Johnson, was there. We had prowled the streets of Toxteth and the south end of Liverpool together and was known as 'The Bear' when I was known as 'The Silver Fox'. Mike was with his wife Sylvia, one of Carol's oldest friends, and their two children Lindsay and Chris. I have a soft spot for Lindsay who is my God-daughter and well capable of twisting me around her little finger.

Of the gifts I received, the one that meant the most was a cut-glass decanter bearing an inscribed silver label.

To the Boss
From all your colleagues
on the Wirral Crime Squad
August 1984 to February 1989

I was very flattered, but learned later that Ron and Ben had done the collecting. I didn't know many people who would refuse their appeals for donations. The decanter is at present in my home and will one day be passed to my niece Amanda. She is married to a barrister, Gary Reynolds, so in the fullness of time it may well end up in his chambers. I think in some way that is quite appropriate.

One more person arrived at the celebrations who I was not expecting, Richard Adams. I was delighted that he had made the effort to come and be with me on my special night. I thought it was very typical of him.

During my time on the Wirral Crime Squad an independent survey revealed that approximately 50% of reported burglaries were committed by drug addicts. A young woman admitted to me that over a period of two-and-a-years she was personally responsible for shoplifting in excess of £100,000 worth of goods. It was nearly all spent on heroin.

This enormous cost is passed on to the customer by way of increased prices and inflated insurance premiums. If the cost of policing, putting offenders through the judicial system and keeping them in prison is added, it is easy to recognise that the price we all pay for heroin addiction is enormous.

And this does not take into account the social cost. In 1995, a survey calculated that on Merseyside alone the annual turnover in illegal drug trading was £252,000,000, which is close to three-quarters-of-a-million pounds a day! The county has double the national average for drug trafficking arrests and a rate of unlawful possession of illegal substances, 55% above the figures for the rest of the country. More recently, guns have been introduced onto the streets of Liverpool and Manchester and many other towns and cities.

The drug ecstasy has entered the dance club scene on a huge scale and yet heroin remains the primary drug of the street. There have been many police innovations and the battle goes on, but there is not the slightest indication that the police, the courts or the government are any closer to resolving this massive social problem.

Police and Customs officers have made spectacular arrests and seized millions of pounds worth of drugs. As far as the public are concerned, however, it is on the streets and estates where the problem must be tackled. Taking on the drug barons in the Golden Triangle or wherever is all part of the battle, but it is in our towns and cities where the fight must be the most intensive. As far as local dealers are concerned, I am convinced that the only way to deal with their problem is to adopt the principle used in New York which has shown early signs of making a significant impression: zero tolerance.

From my own experience, I have seen concentrated policing work. It must, however, be supported by the local communities, local authorities, the courts and the government.

The people of this country are sick of having their homes burgled, their cars stolen and their handbags and wallets snatched. For too long this has been a part of our lives. People are scared of the deadly menace drugs bring into our homes. Parents are terrified of their children being caught up in it.

How far does it have to go? How much do

people have to tolerate? How far do standards have to fall before something serious is done?

For many, it is already too late, but for the future of our children we have a moral obligation to act now.

More police and specialised resources must be made available in every area where the problem exists. For addicted dealers there must be a rehabilitation programme available to them as part of a punitive sentence. If they do not co-operate with the programme, imprisonment is the only alternative. The choice is theirs.

The first move must and can only come from the government. If the political will exists to confront this issue, and surely to God it does, then there must be an immediate declaration that the resources are to be made available.

With the recent change in government, this could be the time for a minister to be appointed whose sole responsibility is to co-ordinate the fight against the drug dealers. He or she need not be a professional politician, but must be pragmatic and realistic in their approach. It requires someone who can grasp the root of the problem and has the necessary experience to be able to address the relevant issues.

From the first day of my command of the Wirral Crime Squad, I had displayed on my desk a quotation from George Bernard Shaw that John F Kennedy had similarly mounted in the Oval

Office during his tenure in the White House. It reads:

> *Some men see things as they are and say why?*
> *I dream of things that never were and say why*
>   *not?*

Perhaps it is too much to hope that we could ever completely eradicate drug abuse. I believe we have a duty to try and say to ourselves *'why not?'*

The early evening of 30th January, just a few weeks before my promotion date, found me with Ben and Ron in an unmarked car parked in a darkened side street off Mount Pleasant Road in Wallasey. Divisional officers had just received some disturbing information about a man who was shortly expected at the address we were watching.

His wife had reported that he had firearms in the house and had recently been acting strangely, even threatening to kill her. There had been no time to organise firearms officers and they had asked we give them back up. They were parked a short distance away, covering the other end of the road. The hastily contrived plan was to see who was the nearest when he arrived, and to take him out before he could gain access.

We stiffened as we saw the headlights of

his vehicle as he drove towards us, and he manoeuvred into the kerb immediately adjacent to our car. Alighting, he crossed the short pavement and was about to put his key in the door as we approached. Ron identified us as police officers and immediately he tried to push past us. As he did so a firearm clattered to the floor from his overalls. Ron and I slammed him against a wall, Ben dived for the gun and retrieved it. It was a loaded .22 pistol.

When we returned to Wallasey we were all in a silent, contemplative mood. Speaking for myself I'd had one hell of a shock. We went to the bar and I ordered a round of drinks. Even Ron, who rarely drank, took one off me gratefully. He took a long swig, looked at us and smiled, shaking his head. I knew what was in his mind. It could have been any one of us.

"You know, boss," Ben said, immediately lightening the atmosphere, "your Carol would have killed us if you hadn't got to Birkenhead."

EPILOGUE

In five years I had come full circle, posted once again to my beloved Birkenhead, but this time in a new uniform and with an extra pip on my shoulder. I parked my car in the allocated garage at one end of the yard and entered the station just after eight o'clock in the morning.

Three young officers watched by their sergeant, Bob Jones, a legend at Birkenhead, leapt to their feet and bade me 'good morning'. Bob welcomed me to the station. This fuss was the normal procedure for the arrival of a senior officer but I wasn't entirely comfortable with it.

In time gone by, Birkenhead had been a borough force and as I walked into my richly carpeted and furnished office I could see, very faintly, beneath several layers of paint, the words 'Deputy Chief Constable'. I was used to a far more modest working environment, but thought that I could probably get used to it. Jane Clement, who ran the administration unit and who I had known for a long time, brought me a coffee and we shared a joke about my new accommodation. I was left on my own and sat back to take it all in. Nothing but pleasant thoughts crossed my mind. My days with the Wirral Crime Squad were now behind me and I was now in the pleasant routine of nine 'til five and most weekends at home with Carol. This was the life. My daydreams were interrupted by a knock on the door and before I could answer, it opened and Arthur Cowley walked in. He took a quick look around the office.

"Nice office, Boss," he said before shoving some papers into my hand. "Look, we got another bleedin' 'not guilty' verdict at the Crown on Thursday! Not guilty! I ask you! What are we supposed to do? He was bang to rights, I tell you, absolutely bang . . ."

And so life goes on.

APPENDIX 1

Detective Chief Inspector Mike Mulloy Commendations and Awards

18 June 1964
    Chief Constable's commendation for most excellent work in crime detection.

28 August 1965
    Chief Constable's commendation for excellent work in the detection of crime.

26 July 1967
    Chief Constable's commendation for outstanding work in the detection and prevention of crime.

24 Nov 1969
    Chief Constable's commendation for outstanding work in the detection of crime.

30 March 1971	Chief Constable's commendation for outstanding record of arrests in the detection of serious crime.
22 May 1972	Chief Constable's commendation for outstanding work in the detection of serious crimes.
26 Sept 1972	Granted the Police Authority Award of Merit for outstanding work and devotion to duty displayed in the detection of serious crime, including the arrest of a male who had committed over 300 robberies and smashing a gang who were responsible for over 100 burglaries.
4 Jan 1974	Chief Constable's commendation for excellent work in the detection of crime whilst a member of the Regional Crime Squad.
5 August 1974	Judge's commendation by the Recorder of Liverpool, His Honour Mr Justice Lyons, for intelligent work in cases of serious burglaries.
11 March 1975	Chief Constable's commendation for outstanding leadership of a Special Robbery Squad in Toxteth.

3 Dec 1975	Chief Constable's commendation for excellent work in the case of a murder of a six year old girl.
11 July 1976	Judge's commendation by His Honour Mr Justice Lawton for work in a complicated conspiracy and theft enquiry and the eventual arrest of thirty-six offenders.
15 Feb 1977	Detective Chief Superintendent's commendation for outstanding work in a case of armed robbery and the arrests of five offenders.
25 Jan 1978	Chief Constable's commendation for outstanding performance in the field of crime detection, whilst a member of the Serious Crime Squad, and in particular for excellent work in cases of armed robbery.
26 June 1979	Judge's commendation by His Honour, Mr Justice Price, for work leading to arrests for burglary and handling stolen goods.
25 July 1979	Chief Superintendent's commendation for interest, determination and attention

to duty, leading to the convictions of persons for burglary, theft and receiving.

10 Oct 1979   Commended by the Wirral Justices for utmost efficiency and courage in a case of serious public disorder.

9 Dec 1981   Chief Superintendent's commendation for the efficient, patient and entirely professional way an injured and mentally disturbed young woman who was showing violent tendencies was dealt with.

4 Jan 1982   Certificate of Merit awarded by the Royal Society for the Prevention of Cruelty to Animals in recognition of the action during the rescue of an alsation dog from an attic in a derelict house, under dangerous conditions.

16 Dec 1982   Letter of commendation from the Liverpool Shipwreck and Humane Society for the successful rescue of several persons from a burning car, which was in danger of exploding.

27 April 1983	Chief Superintendent's commendation for intelligent and most professional policing during an exercise which resulted in the arrest of a determined escapee from prison.
26 July 1983	Judge's commendation by His Honour, Mr Justice Lawton, for conduct throughout the whole case of perjury and attempt to pervert the course of justice and for preventing a miscarriage of justice.
17 August 1983	Chief Superintendent's commendation for skill and initiative in a number of criminal cases involving a male, later dealt with at Liverpool Crown Courts.
8 Sept 1983	Chief Constable's commendation for courage, skill and determination in disarming an emotionally unstable woman in possession of a carving knife and who was holding two social workers against their will with the weapon.
27 Jan 1984	Awarded HM The Queen's Long Service and Good Conduct Medal.

1 Feb 1984
Chief Superintendent's commendation for excellent team work, initiative and professionalism resulting in an impressive number of arrests for crime.

9 April 1987
Chief Constable's commendation for professionalism and application to duty, resulting in the recovery of a large amount of drugs for importation and the arrest to conviction of determined criminals who were sentenced to long terms of imprisonment. A letter of thanks was also received from HM Customs and Excise.

17 March 1987
Judge's commendation by His Honour Mr Justice Temple, the Recorder of Liverpool, for the assistance given to the courts in a case of armed robbery.

12 Nov 1987
Chief Superintendent's commendation for good work in a serious case of indecency involving young boys.

24 Feb 1988
Judge's commendation by His Honour Mr Justice Naylor for the painstaking investigations leading

to the arrests in a serious case of drug trafficking in Operation Chepstow.

8 August 1988   Judge's commendation by His Honour Mr Justice Nance for the tremendous amount of work entailed in a serious drug trafficking case, namely Operation Brynmoss.

20 Jan 1989   Judge's commendation by His Honour Mr Justice Arthur for the patient, skilful and accomplished work in a major drugs conspiracy, namely Operation Bedford.

27 Oct 1989   Judge's commendation by His Honour Mr Justice Lachs for the successful prosecution of a determined gang of drug suppliers, namely Operation Steeple.

9 May 1991   Chief Constable's commendation for investigative skills, professionalism and determination during an operation which led to the arrest of many offenders for serious offences of supply of hard drugs.

9 May 1991   Chief Constable's commendation
                for determination, initiative and
                dedication to duty, displayed
                whilst conducting complex
                enquiries into numerous drug
                dealings known as 'Dial-a-Smack',
                which resulted in the conviction
                of a team of highly organised
                criminals.

9 May 1991   Chief Constable's commendation
                for devotion to duty, good
                observations and interrogative
                skills displayed during an
                operation which led to the arrest
                of many offenders who dealt in
                hard drugs, involving over
                £500,000, and sentenced to long
                terms of imprisonment.

9 May 1991   Chief Constable's commendation
                for leadership, surveillance and
                professionalism displayed during
                an operation, which became one
                of the largest drug investigations
                leading to the closure of a drugs
                network and the successful
                convictions of many of its
                members.

9 May 1991   Chief Constable's commendation
                for professionalism, skill and

dedication to duty displayed in
the investigation of drug-related
offences, which resulted in the
conviction of one Merseyside's
most violent and criminally
prolific individuals.

APPENDIX 2

**Members of the Wirral Crime Squad
6th August 1984 – 6th February 1989**

Sgt 4498 Dave Ackersley
PC 6141 Peter Allerston
DC 3445 Frank Anderson
PC 6520 Terry Barnes
PC 5856 Ian Beaumont
Sgt 3107 Derek Bebbington
DC 3447 Peter Blythe
PC 5195 Steve Brookes
PC 5917 Dougie Brown
Sgt 3530 Mike Carr
PC 3314 Ron Cashin
PC 6488 Peter Challinor
PC 7446 Brian Charlton
PC 7141 Graham Clarke
PC 6550 Mark Clemson
DC 4566 Martin Colton
PC 7354 Dave Connor

PC 4783 Arthur Cowley
PC 5770 Mike Craven
DS 2800 Elmore Davies
Sgt 2779 Phil Davie
PC 7215 Joe Danher
PC 5497 Phil Dobbing
DS 3873 Derek East
PW 5980 Di Ethelstone
PW 7239 Joy Eakins
PC 4271 Paul Fearon
PC 5827 Jimmy Forrest
PC 6431 Sean Gallagher
PC 7188 Mark Gerrard
PC 5299 Kenny Gilmour
PC 6289 Dave Gregson
PC 6425 Al Green
PC 5644 Tommy Gunn
DC 3315 Ron Hankey
PW 7004 Sybil Hardacre
PC 5347 Paul Healey
PC 6611 Paul Heslop
DC 3981 Geoff Higgs
Sgt 3337 Peter Horn
PC 6552 Greg Hunt
DS 2762 Bob Hughes
DS 2616 Peter Jones
Sgt 5117 Bob Jones
Sgt 5359 Alan Jones
PC 7166 Maurice Jones
PC 6466 Barry Jones

PC 6426 Neil Johnston
DS 3155 Tony Jopson
PC 6676 Sean Kehoe
PC 4474 George Kettle
Sgt 2804 Joe Large
PC 3443 Paul Lathom
PC 6778 Ian Latimer
Sgt 3495 Terry Leach
PW 5566 Les Leddington
PC 7005 Phil Leach
PC 6469 Richie Lewis
PC 7328 Frank Liston
PC 6305 Steve Littlejohn
PW 5305 Joan Lomax
PC 5301 Steve Longrigg
PC 6290 Colin Matthews
PC 5931 Mike McDonough
PC 6046 Dave McGarvie
PC 5859 Mike McMahon
PC 6492 Dave Mitchell
PC 6378 Mike Morgan
PC 6490 Billy Morris
Insp1933 Mike Mulloy
PC 5862 Ben O'Brien
PC 5605 Paddy O'Mahoney
PC 3342 Dave Owens
PC 6050 Mike Parkinson
PC 6556 Richie Penston
Sgt 3041 Stan Preston
PC 3073 Steve Quayle

PC 5986 Mike Rimmer
PC 5016 Charlie Roughley
DC 2799 Al Rushton
PC 5531 John Smith
PC 5221 Frank Sherratt
PC 6253 Andy Stewart
DC 5364 Frank Thomas
PC 6179 Peter Thomas
PC 5731 Craig Thompson
PC 3691 Dennis Tyndall
PW 5359 Julie Wallace-Jones
DS 2479 Tommy Webb
PC 6494 Richie Whitworth
PW 6524 Mandy Weisenecker
PC 4986 Alan Wilkes
DC 5434 Steve Williams
PC 6105 Mark Wilson
PC 6429 Phil Wright

The following Drug Squad officers were directly involved in Wirral Crime Squad operations: DS Keith Raybould, DC Graham Gathercole, DC Brendan Farrell, DC Kenny Johnson, DS Alan Jones and DS Neil Hamilton.